SCENES FROM THE P

MANCHES

RAILWAY TERMINI

Manchester Central 12th May 1959 British Rail

E. M. JOHNSON

Author's Note: This third printing of my original 1987 volume has given me the opportunity to revise some previous captions and add a slice of new, hitherto unpublished, material. In the intervening six years Manchester's remaining termini have altered yet again: trackwork and platforms at Piccadilly were partly remodelled in the Autumn of 1988, whilst Victoria station is currently undergoing a massive upheaval pending the erection of an arena complex. Links between these two termini have been made at last following the inauguration of the long-awaited Metrolink in 1992. Piccadilly now has a new signalling centre and the May of this year saw the opening of direct services to Manchester Airport; the airport station itself becoming the city's latest terminal.

E.M. Johnson. Burnage. September 1993.

Copyright C 1987 Foxline Publishing. Reprinted 1989. Third Edition 1993.
ISBN 1 870119 30 4

Designed and Edited by Gregory K. Fox.
Printed by Amadeus Press, Huddersfield.
Published by Foxline Publishing
32 Urwick Road, Romiley, Stockport. SK6 3JS

Manchester — Ancoats, 15th May 1922. The names of Manchester's passenger termini such as Central and London Road readily spring to mind. Lesser-known but of equal importance were several conveniently placed goods stations helping to serve the city's everyday needs. The sites and some of the buildings survive in varying forms but transport development in recent times has seen to it that none are served by rail. One that has disappeared almost without trace is Ancoats on the east side of the city. Situated at the junction of Adair Street and Great Ancoats Street in what was once a teeming manufacturing area, this large depot was opened by the Midland Railway on 2nd May 1870. By way of its tripartite involvement in the Cheshire Lines organisation, the Midland had direct access to Liverpool whereas the Midlands, London and Scotland could be reached over the company's own lines. This view from the St. Andrews Square side of the depot shows the yard with a varied assortment of horse-drawn vehicles and illustrates contemporary practices in goods handling, with mixed consignments utilizing barrels, crates and boxes awaiting distribution. To the right of the picture, the name of Bass, Ratcliff and Gretton serves to remind us of the importance attached to rail distribution by the Burton-on-Trent based brewery. Until the late 1950's no fewer than twenty-nine trains left the East Midlands town nightly for destinations throughout the country, and serving Manchester. *Photo: National Railway Museum*

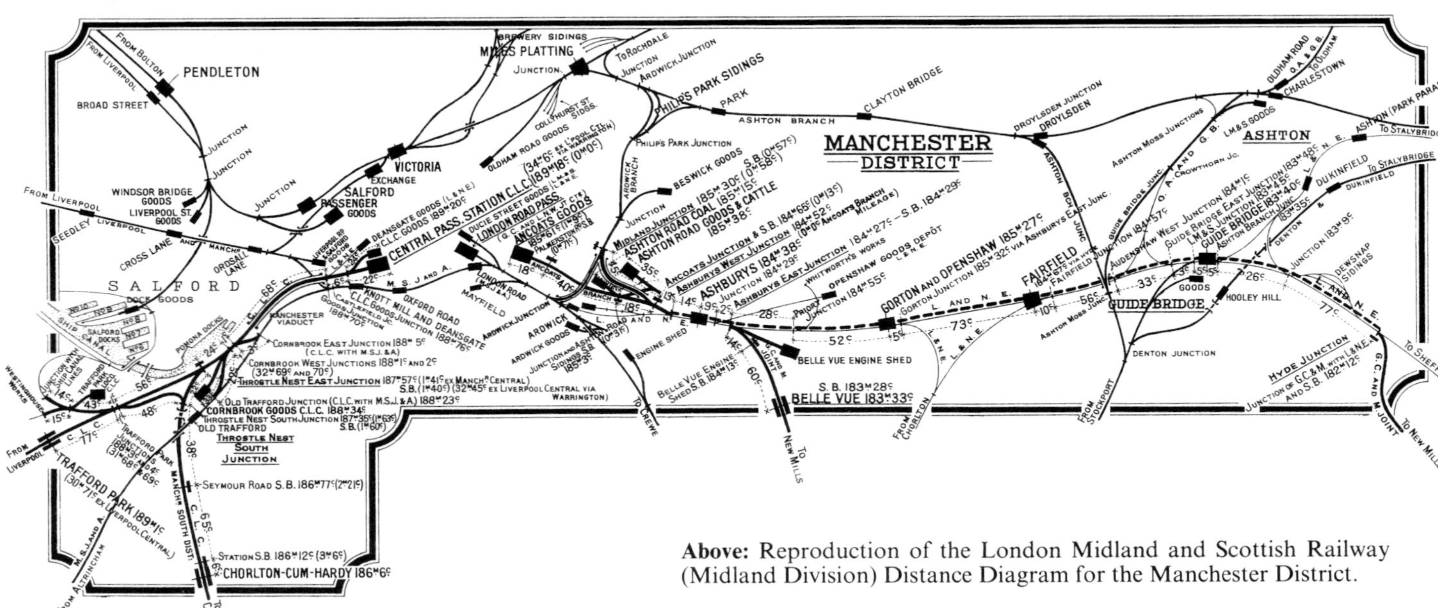

Above: Reproduction of the London Midland and Scottish Railway (Midland Division) Distance Diagram for the Manchester District.

ntroduction

 was well over 150 years ago in the dawn of the reign of William IV that Manchester established itself as one of the first cities in the world to be served by a railway. The tory of that first venture, the Liverpool and Manchester Railway, has become somewhat trite in recent years at the expense perhaps of later developments and other spects of Manchester's railway history. For although the L&M was of momentous importance in the historic sense, its place in the jigsaw of the area's railway eography has ultimately become relatively minor. Other routes were later to connect the two cities and ironically a canal which was later to take back a considerable mount of the freight traffic that the railway was built to convey. Movement of the freight was the raison d'etre of Manchester's first railway. Traffic in cotton had established the city as the *Cottonopolis* of the Victorian era and looking at the wholesale manufacture of this commodity in the mills of the surrounding Lancashire towns, the umerous factories, coal mines, warehouses and not least, the people of the area, we have the foundations of Manchester's evolution as a major railway centre.

That initial route from Liverpool, followed closely by successful ventures from Birmingham and Leeds, quickly established Manchester's regional importance. The mitations of Liverpool Road, Oldham Road and to some extent, London Road, were highlighted as the railways grew unabated. Out of this early development came ne embryo of the two large city stations, Victoria, to work the Lancashire and Yorkshire interests, and London Road to cement the base for southbound activities. The esultant railway activity in the city boundary therefore fell into two broad areas, centering on Victoria, which catered for east and west traffic and connecting Yorkshire nd the North-East with Warrington, Liverpool and North Wales, and a second at London Road where the ever powerful London and North Western Railway had set ut its stall to challenge for the lucrative London and Midlands business alongside the Manchester, Sheffield and Lincolnshire organization. Any stability that had been ought was quickly placed under pressure, particularly from the expansionist policies of the Midland Railway, forever on the lookout for new territories to conquer. Its enture through the Derbyshire dales and over the near one thousand feet summit at Peak Forest enabled the Manchester goal to be reached but dissatisfaction with nared facilities ultimately resulted in the creation of a large goods depot at Ancoats and the passenger terminal at Central, courtesy of the Cheshire Lines Committee. part from the opening of Exchange in 1884 by the LNWR, which was effectively an enlargement of Victoria, the network in and around the city was by and large omplete. The railways continued to expand, albeit at a more conservative rate, Mayfield station being the last link in an eighty year chain which saw the creation of assenger stations which became *Manchester's Railway Termini*.

In the fuller railway sense, in and around the city at one time or another were once established several locomotive works, a carriage building works, an abundance of ngine sheds, extensive dock, colliery and industrial lines and some of the largest and most impressive goods depots in the country. Indeed, Manchester – for its sins – as once the only city outside London that possessed four railway termini, historical events and complications forcing them to remain outside the city centre to their ltimate detriment.

As elsewhere, changes in the social and industrial climate over the last 25 years, coupled with the much-needed modernisation of our railway system, have wrought any alterations to Manchester's rail network. In this little essay in the "Scenes from the Past" series I have endeavoured to show something of the railway scenario in is part of the world in what now seem far-off days. As we once said: "The past is another country"; let us, briefly, journey there.

cknowledgements

ny work of this nature relies heavily on its picture content and I think I have been more fortunate than most in having had an excellent choice of material from which to noose. In particular, I would like to thank Brian Green whose photographs must rank as some of the finest ever taken in this area. In a similar vein, Bill Johnson, aymond Keeley, Michael Mensing and Martin Welch have all provided superb pictures from their collections.

Thanks are due also to Ronnie Gee for his photographs and comments on workings at (what was then) London Road, to my old friend Ray Hepner for the kind loan photographs, maps and timetables. Others who have given freely of their help and photographs are: V. R. Anderson, C. A. Appleton, J. M. Bentley, R. G. Chapman, ordon Coltas, J. D. Darby. J. Hammond, John Hooper, Brian Hilton, Mrs. K. Platt (for the kind use of her late husband, Geoffrey's material), The National Railway luseum, W. G. Rear.

I must also offer a big 'thank-you' to my wife Mary, who has had to put up with what must have seemed like an endless sea of paper and photographs over the last two ears or so. Final thanks go to Greg Fox who, apart from giving me the opportunity to publish this book, has generously given help with maps, architectural and other etails.

E. M. Johnson, Burnage, Manchester. October, 1987.

elow: Manchester Central, 12th May 1959 *Photo: British Rail*

1. Manchester London Road, 24th May 1901. Mounted police, an excited crowd and an event uppermost in the public's mind form the canvas for our first picture – taken in the earliest days of the Edwardian era. Few events in the latter part of the 19th and early 20th centuries had fuelled the country's imagination as much as the Boer War. A huge crowd has gathered at London Road to watch the Volunteers of the Manchester Regiment (Ardwicks) on the last part of their journey back from South Africa. The troops had travelled to Manchester from Ashton Barracks. Perhaps war-weary, they were in no doubt relieved to be home and pleased with the £5 bounty each had received on assembly at Ashton. Rain was obviously in the air, witness the raised umbrellas, a necessary appendage too on top of the Great Central's horse-drawn buses. *Photo: R. G. Chapman Collection*

2. London Road. It is twenty minutes to five in the afternoon and all the hustle and bustle of Edwardian Manchester is seen around London Road station approach in this view from the corner of Auburn Street. The date of the photograph is unknown but almost certainly post-1901, determined by the presence of electric tramcars albeit still of the open top variety. The motor car has yet to make its presence felt and it will be a generation or more before the horse drawn cabs relinquish their hold on passenger trade. To the left is the capacious goods station of the London and North Western Railway Company, backdrop to the proliferation of advertising hoardings The Gaiety Theatre is to host from the 11th May, "The Return of the Prodigal" by St. John Hankin. One is left in no doubt about the benefits of Stephens Gum, Epp's Cocoa, H. Samuel's Watches and Brook's Grains of Health Salt as these and many other signs almost demand the attention of passers-by. Of gastronomic interest are the "Fish Teas" at 9d and 4-course meals for one shilling (5p) to be had at the Grotto Cafes in Stevenson Square, Ridgefield and Princess Street. *Photo: G. K. Fox Collection*

3. London Road. High above the blackened stonework of the offices and booking-hall the Union Jack flutters proudly as flags and bunting proclaim the 1937 coronation of King George VI and Queen Elizabeth. No actual date is given for this postcard view but judging by the activity on the station approach, maybe a summer Bank Holiday is in full swing, the clock suggesting early afternoon departures. A good variety of pre-war cars line the sides of the approach roads, each one appearing in the all-pervading black of those years. Observant readers will have spotted the shafts of the horse-drawn carts projecting above the boundary wall of the two goods yards. Alongside is evidence of London Road's twin status in the form of the LMS and LNER poster hoardings. Beneath the electric light standard is an advert proclaiming the virtues of what were then delicately described as "Surgical Appliances" by a well-known local company. Displayed across the front of the booking-hall canopy are the names of a variety of places served by the two railways and include the West of England, Bournemouth, the South Coast and Cromer. This was ever a favourite railway device, even if some of the associations were a little tenuous! Notice the large placard advertising the Daily Dispatch, one of the Manchester-based Kemsley Newspaper's publications, a name now consigned to the nation's history books.
Photo: G. K. Fox Collection

4. Manchester Victoria c.1910. Unlike its neighbours at London Road and Central, Victoria Station's development had evolved almost on a piecemeal basis since its opening in 1844. The final phase of alteration and rebuilding, completed in 1909, saw the number of platforms increased to seventeen making it one of the largest stations in the country. The view here illustrates platform 12 looking in an easterly direction. This side of the station was developed on these lines in 1884, although the numbering of the platforms latterly followed the rebuilding of 1903. Reconstruction in 1993 saw the complete obliteration of this part of the station to make way for an operation more suited to current requirements.
Author's collection.

5. Manchester Victoria, c. 1925. It is only in recent years that the frontage of Victoria Station has been revealed to its full extent. Appreciation of the Dawes facade was limited by the offices on Hunts Bank from where this view is taken. Out of the picture to the left is the original 1844 station which ran parallel with what is now platform eleven. The entrance to the stations restaurant and grill room remind us of the opulence of the period although the "Smoke Room" might perhaps be not so welcomed nowadays. The large overall canopy to the right performed a most useful function until one of its supporting columns was hit by a bus in 1937, causing the roof to sag and resulting in the structure's removal. Much refurbishment has been carried out over the last few years although the retraction of facilities in general has reduced the desired effectiveness. *Photo: V. R. Anderson Collection*

6. Manchester Exchange, c. 1905. Long skirts, straw Boaters and horse-drawn vehicles add touches of Edwardian spice to this lunchtime view across Victoria Street and up the Cathedral Approach to Manchester's Exchange Station. Opened in 1884 by the LNWR, the station drew its name from the close proximity of the Cotton Exchange at a time when Manchester was one of the world's major trading centres in that commodity. In effect, a westerly extension of Victoria where the LNW had shared joint tenure with the L&Y, Exchange provided the company with a further 5 platforms spread over five and a half acres for their exclusive use, overcrowding and subsequent congestion having got steadily worse at Victoria. Built by Robert Neil & Sons in the Italian style, problems had been encountered during construction owing to the necessity to bridge the Irwell in two places. Clues to destinations served by Exchange are provided by the hoardings, boat traffic in particular being keenly sought by the various railway companies. Notice that electric traction has yet to arrive to power the city's trams and certainly the veteran motor-car is the only example of the species in sight.
Photo: G. K. Fox Collection

7. Midland Hotel, c. 1910. It was perhaps only natural that a company which placed such high store on passenger comfort should have produced Manchester's best known, and at one time most sumptuous hotel. Seen here in pre-First War days, the Midland stands on a site between Lower Mosley Street and Mount Street and is flanked on one side by St. Peter's Square and on the other by the erstwhile Central Station, to which it was once connected. A school and two concert halls were demolished to make way for the hotel which opened for business in 1900, its marble exterior and plush interior rapidly becoming a focus for the higher echelons of the business fraternity. It was at the Midland in May 1904 that the historic meeting between Messrs. Rolls and Royce took place and from which this was to lead to the production of the legendary cars in nearby Hulme. Interestingly, F. H. Royce had served 3 years of a Premium Apprenticeship on the Great Northern Railway at Peterborough from 1874 before foresaking his railway career for that of the automotive industry. The Midland lost its railway ownership some years ago and has now undergone complete refurbishment at the hands of an American concern. Could just a touch of irony be detected here?

Photo: G. K. Fox Collection

8. Manchester Central, c. 1910. The forecourt of Central in the early years of the century with the names of the joint owners prominently displayed across the frontage. The verandah to the right extended across the forecourt and over Windmill Street to the rear of the Midland Hotel. The plan to build a hotel immediately in front of the station and to rid the site of its "temporary" facilities came to nought. An early motor car can be seen beneath the verandah but horse drawn transport, along with the electric tram, still dominate. A clue to the date of the photograph is provided by the existence on the left of the extensions housing platforms 8 and 9, built parallel to Lower Mosley Street in 1906.

Photo: Railway Revivals Collection

9. Manchester Central. A piece of 'thirties history and what might be termed the classic view of Manchester Central. Flanking the station's cobbled approach is a line of pre-war cars, all doubtless robed in sombre black; their flat windscreens, polished chrome headlamps and trim well to the fore. Where are you now, one wonders, BBU 720 and OXT 937? The special bus in the then familiar Corporation livery of red and white, is obviously waiting for a number of Service personnel. How formal the crew look in their uniforms and peaked caps! An interesting touch is provided by the "Royal Mail" van and we mustn't forget the hoarding advertising Picture Post, quite the most famous illustrated magazine in the country at the time.

Photo: G. K. Fox Collection

10. Manchester London Road, 25th January 1955. The wide but rather uninspiring approach allowed an excellent view of the 1866 building designed by Mills and Murgatroyd to replace the earlier Store Street Station. The opening of the Travis Street station in 1840 saw the Manchester and Birmingham Railway enter the town from the south albeit only as far as Heaton Norris. In 1841 it was to accommodate trains of the Sheffield, Ashton-under-Lyne and Manchester Company, a situation that was to continue for some years until enlargement became necessary as business and the railway network expanded. The original promoters the M & B, had been taken over by the LNWR in 1846 and the new station was located in its present position but with many additional platforms of which three, on the east side, were for the sole use of the Manchester, Sheffield and Lincolnshire Railway Company by which name it had become known. The station, although operated jointly, was owned by the LNWR, but also contained the headquarters of the MS&L until the thrust south by the company, renamed as the Great Central Railway, took them to Marylebone Road in London. To the left of the picture, the erstwhile LNWR goods warehouse can be seen but of possibly greater interest is the presence on the approach of a Rolls-Royce taxi, registration number GK 8374, prestigious travel indeed!

Photo: British Rail

11. London Road, 28th June 1950. Few photographs have come to light showing the station buildings in detail and one suspects that architectural photography was not a high priority of the railway photographer. One of a series taken in June 1950, this view shows the eastern side of the station which gave rather restricted access to the platforms serving the former GCR lines to Sheffield, Hayfield etc. Booking arrangements were almost apologetic compared with those of the LNWR and one is left in no doubt about the distinction between landlord and tenant. The elevated position of the building enhanced its attractiveness and whether demolition was strictly necessary is open to question, especially when the imposing facades of the former cotton warehouses along Portland Street, now internally modernised, are studied. Whatever the reason, there was much duplication of facilities in the old building and a much more spacious and functional station resulted from the re-building. Of interest are the stone setts, quickly discarded but now finding favour in pedestrianized precincts and the like.

Photo: R. G. Chapman Collection

12. London Road, 22 July 1959. Entering the station by the eastern side booking hall/corridor presented the passengers with this somewhat uninviting view. To those who were familiar with the station in the nineteen fifties, scenes such as this now seem light years away from the present terrazzoed concourse. To enable comparison with today's arrangements, the further of the two refreshment rooms occupies the site of the booking hall. Similarly, the Wymans bookstall shares approximately the same location as the Menzies outlet who, incidentally look over the former in 1969. The roadway "in" and "out" of the station marked the demarcation between the separate railway undertakings. The far side functioned under the auspices of the former LMS (LNWR) regime whereas the nearside was the territory of the LNER (GCR). After the 1948 nationalization of course, the Midland and Eastern regions continued the tradition. Is the gentleman to the left pondering on the attractiveness of a trip to Blackpool, fare 7/- (35p)?

Photo: British Rail

13. London Road, 26th June 1950. At the top of the station approach, this time on the western side, the smoke-blackened features of the main building dominates the surroundings. The main vehicular access to the station extends to the right providing a protective roofing over the parcels area. It is surprising to note that the parcels van just inside the entrance is a horse drawn type. For the moment there appears to be no parking problems under the verandah but no less than six porters are in attendance for the next rush of passengers. Above the station name is a hoarding which historically has advertised the newspapers of the Kemsley organisation. Located in Withy Grove, close to Victoria Station, the company produced many popular titles, one of which was the Evening Chronicle, a popular tabloid that disappeared in the 1960's, victim of absorption by the rival Evening News.

Photo: Kemsley Studios

14. London Road, 26th June 1950. Delicately cast ironwork and scrolled supporting columns are noteworthy focal points in this view beneath the verandah adjacent to the former LNWR booking hall entrance. The posters are an interest in themselves and reveal much in respect of train services at the time. From London Road, Restaurant Car facilities were available on nine weekday expresses to Euston as opposed to three on the ex GC route via Sheffield to Marylebone. Excursion traffic was still very popular and day return trips were available to Burnley (3/9d), Derby (7/6d), Hellifield (6/3d) and Llandudno (10/6d). The details of bus services to other Manchester stations indicated the almost splendid isolation in which London Road found itself, a situation which may never be resolved unless some form of cross-city rail system is promoted. *Photo: Kemsley Studios*

15. (Below left) London Road, June 1951. Stepping inside the former LNWR/LMS booking hall three and a half years after nationalization, we see the familiar maroon coloured enamelled London Midland Region signs which have just been fixed although the fares lists still bear the "LMS" legend in the corner. Discernable examples are Stockport (3rd Class single, 1/3d), Styal (3rd Class return, 2/9d), Bournemouth (1st Class return, 99/5d) and London (1st Class return, 75/-). All the fine panelled woodwork and ornate ceiling would be associated with a stately home rather than a railway station, reminding us of the many architectural slendours of our railway heritage. The quest for progress has seen the loss of so much but fortunately examples such as the Manchester and Birmingham Railway coat of arms, seen here above the First Class ticket window, have been preserved, in this instance on the front of the Piccadilly Station building. The modernization of this ticket office in 1954 resulted in the closure of the booking office on the eastern side.

Photo: British Rail

.6. **(Above) London Road, 22nd July 1959.** Again in the booking ıall but on this occasion looking into the station. In an ıtmosphere of almost regal Victoriana, the "Empire" kiosk eems something of an anachronism but is now history itself.
Photo: British Rail

.7. (right) **Exchange. c.1935.** As mentioned previously the locations ıf London Road and Victoria Stations were as a result of historical ·vents and even as the crow flies, a good three-quarters of a mile eparates them. Over the years, several proposals have been put ·orward in an attempt to link the two; one of the most recent being he "Pic-Vic" tunnel scheme of the 1970's, ruled out because of the ·igh cost. A compromise was the introduction of the "Centreline" ervice, a series of small buses shuttling across town. A predecessor ıf this "innovation" stands at the top of the Exchange station ıpproach whilst about to be overtaken by a similar type of vehicle ·ound for Central Station.
G.M.T. Society.

.8. **(Centre-Right) London Road, c. 1931.** platform end view on the LNER side of he station showing an excursion notice. Aore important however are the large ·etters above the hoarding which iden-·ified the platforms in such a way to ·istinguish them from their LMS neigh-·ours . The three platforms were lettered ·, B and C. London Road was literally wo stations in one with virtually all ervices, i.e. offices, goods facilities, ocomotive arrangements, etc, being ·uplicated. The separation was enforced ·y iron railings running the length of the ·tation in a position approximately where he edge of the present platform is con-tructed. A cobbled roadway was ·rovided on the GC/LNE side of the ·ailings.
Photo: R. G. Chapman Collection

.9. **London Road, 22nd July 1959.** This ·cene can be encapsulated in the well ·nown phrase "all human life is there". A ·plendid essay in candid photography on ·e station concourse adjacent to the end ·f platform 4, few of this incredibly varied ·rowd appears to be aware of being ·aptured on film. The impending ·odernization and rebuilding pro-·ramme saw this as London Road's last ·ummer in its old form whilst the chalked ·essage on the right advises helpfully ·at a certain train from London *will be ·ubject to some delay*, old habits die ·ard!
Photo: British Rail

20. London Road. January 1953. Although daylight is visible at the end of the roof, electric lights shine brightly over platforms 3 and 4. This was a January day and it is quite likely to have been a foggy one - though, thankfully, such things are now only a memory. Flagstones glisten in the damp winter air in this scene, one rich in a flavour that only a large railway station could possess. Standing out clearly are the huge iron columns supporting the roof of the Victorian trainshed, splendid features still visible today of course. An interesting aspect of the ex-LMS side of London Road revolves around the platform numbering. To the right of the photographer, across the tracks, was platform 1. Platform 2 disappeared in an earlier rebuilding programme, and the platforms had been re-numbered again by the time the modernisation commenced in 1959. Seat reservations at 1/- (5p) each, and the ever famous "Brylcreem" advertisement are popular contemporary touches, along with posters reminding us to "mind that door" and "label your luggage". These platforms are now numbered 8 and 9 respectively. *British Rail.*

21. London Road, c. 1957. Strong beams of sunlight cascade through London Road's roof to highlight the fine proportions of 'Jubilee' No. 45578 *United Provinces* as she backs out of the terminus towards Longsight in the summer of 1957. Beneath the web of steelwork can be seen part of the station's No 3 signal box affectionately nicknamed 'The Lighthouse' by signalmen; the box standing across platforms 5 and 6 and dating from 1909. It was a small affair housing only 26 levers and used the Webb/Thompson all-electric signalling system deployed throughout the LNW side of the station. *Photo: W. Johnson*

2. **London Road, n.d.** Happy hours spent train spotting at London Road are recalled by Bill Johnson's superb shot of Coronation Class 4-6-2 No. 6256 *Sir William A. Stanier F.R.S* with steam issuing on all fronts, including the coal pusher, as she backs down to collect her train. Judging by the nmaculate condition of the paintwork, the engine is probably ex-Crewe Works after a major overhaul, it being common practice for Pacific types to e "run-in" on local trains between London Road and Crewe and indicated here by the stopping passenger train headcode. Popularly known as Duchesses" No. 46256 was the penultimate member of the class, being turned out from Crewe in 1947 under the auspices of H. G. Ivatt. Subtle ifferences from the Stanier design included a shortened cab, different design of trailing truck and roller bearings, sad perhaps that she did not survive ıto preservation. *Photo: W. Johnson*

3. **London Road, 13th May 1958.** From the lofty heights of No.2 signal box the full panorama across the station throat can be taken in at a glance. To e left the MSJ&A lines, electrified in 1931 to 1500 Volts DC, terminate behind the island platform next to a siding which formerly gave access to the ırntable. Momentarily, the station is quiet, even the simmering Caprotti valve-geared "Black Five" adjacent to the former Great Central signal box iling to create any activity. To the right of the locomotive stand the air reservoirs provided for the pneumatically operated power signalling.

The decades of smoke, steam and soot had taken their toll of the station and the familiar, though begrimed, LNWR pattern corrugated steel signal ms do not readily catch the eye. To the right of the train shed can be seen the warehouses situated between Store Street and Ducie Street. *Photo: British Rail*

24. London Road. The large coupled wheel bosses of No. 45500, "Patriot" betray the locomotive's ancestry. A nominal rebuild of an LNWR "Claughton" class, the wheels and other minor parts had been incorporated into the first two engines to form a class which eventually totalled fifty-two locomotives. This particular locomotive first appeared in 1930 as *Croxteth,* but changed in 1937 to give the class its title. Some enginemen referred to them as "Baby Scots", a pseudonym which the authorities apparently disliked. Seen here at London Road with the stock of a West of England train, *Patriot* was a regular sight at the station during the nineteen fifties been based at Longsight. A colleague from 9A, No. 70033, *Charles Dickens* stands alongside, coaled up and ready to go.

Photo: B. K. B. Green

25. London Road, 16th March 1953. Hauling a rake of express coaching stock out of the station on its way to Longsight is former L&Y 2-4-2 tank engine No. 50705 of Dallam (Warrington) shed. Although taken some five years after nationalization, this fine atmospheric shot defiantly clings to a departed area.

Photo: B. K. B. Green

26. (Below) London Road, 13th May 1958. The photographer on this occasion has journeyed south to avail himself of the high vantage point given from No. 1 signal box. Within a matter of months, the station was to witness alterations on a massive scale to accommodate electrification. Once again hardly a train is in sight to give an almost uninterrupted view of the station approaches. To the left of the picture is Fairfield Street, with trolleybus wires in evidence. The arches at this point once served as stables to many of the horses required for railway use. Today these same arches are leased by the Post Office for general use. The site of Travis Street station, terminus when the lines from the south opened in 1840 were located in a position approximately to the rear of the signal box.

Photo: British Rail

27. London Road, 24th January 1958. This view at London Road presents an almost christmas card like scene, a splendidly pictorial effect which no doubt had the operating authorities cursing! The overhead electric catenary reveals this to be the eastern side of the station, at the end of platform 3 which had previously been designated 'C' to distinguish it from the numbering on the LM side. Breezing over snow-covered points, a 1500 V DC Electric Multiple Unit (later Class 506) runs in from Glossop whilst an A5 Class 4-6-2 tank, popular performers on the GC/MR/NS joint lines to Hayfield and Macclesfield Central, provides a contrast between new and old forms of traction. The coach to the left is standing in the "Horse Dock" road, a facility for end loading and served by the cobbled roadway between platforms 3 and 4. This short line closed on the 3rd February 1960.
Photo: M. S. Welch

28. London Road, 26th June 1957. Successors to the A3 class locomotives on the Marylebone trains as far as Sheffield were the very capable EM2 class Co-Co electrics (later Class 77). Enthusiasts may have regretted the departure of steam from the former GC line services but electrification of the Woodhead route was a very logical step, removing what must have been insufferable footplate conditions through the old Woodhead tunnels. This summer scene sees No. 27005 ready to depart with an express for Sheffield, a journey time of approximately 1 hour. The first two coaches are Gresley teak bodied vehicles, that next to the locomotive being one of the celebrated designer's Buffet Cars. *Photo: B. K. B, Green*

29. London Road, 25th May 1957. A contrast in Eastern Region motive power is provided by the sight of Class A5 tank No. 69822 passing an unidentified EM2 locomotive, the former leaving with a stopping train for Macclesfield Central via Hyde. These 4-6-2 engines were a sturdy and reliable type designed by Mr. J. G. Robinson, the first examples leaving Gorton in 1911 and being perpetuated by Gresley in LNER days. Vintage Great Central tank classes were a well-known feature on the eastern side of London Road, during this period. To the right of the locomotive are the goods lines to Ducie Street, now removed and in use as Piccadilly Station car park.

Photo: B. K. B. Green

30. London Road, 18th May 1954. In the months before the new Woodhead Tunnel was to open, motive power for the Marylebone express was provided on this occasion by Class V2 No. 60878. Some leakage of steam is occurring under the smokebox from steam pipe joints within. Cracks in the "monobloc" cylinder and smokebox saddle casting led to many members of the class being fitted with separate cylinders from 1955 onwards.

Photo: B. K. B. Green

31. London Road, 14th April 1957. Once again we peer across the eastern side tracks of London Road from the No. 2 signal box and see Class C13 No. 67417 pulling away with the empty coaching stock of a Cleethorpes train. Extensive carriage sidings and sheds at Ardwick enabled the servicing of rolling stock from the Eastern Regions services whilst those of the LM were dealt with at Longsight. To the right of the train shed, the conglomeration of goods warehouses of the former GC dominate the background. An ex GC "Pom-Pom" (J11 0-6-0) is engaged as yard shunter while a more modern form of motive power in the shape of Derby "Lightweight" Diesel Multiple Unit enters the station with a local train from Marple. The elevated signal box controlling movements on this side of the station, closed on the 3rd February 1960 as the rebuilding of London Road progressed.

Photo: B. K. B. Green

32. London Road, 25th March 1953. Photographs of goods yard activity are comparatively rare, due no doubt to the predominant interest in the prestige locomotives and passenger trains and to the fact that access to the general public was inevitably restricted. Here we have a splendid view of the former LNWR goods station, adjacent to London Road approach, taken from the offices at the front of the station. The motorway age has not yet arrived and serves as a reminder that the railways were still the major inland carriers. The gabled buildings to the right were both former GCR establishments, the twin gabled structure in the foreground being the Flour warehouse, that to the rear being the six storied "London" warehouse which remains to this day alongside Ducie Street. Next to the brake van on the right is the parapet of the bridge over Store Street whilst most of the site to the left is taken by the building known as Gateway House.
Photo: B. K. B. Green

33. London Road, 25th March 1953. Along the yard, which was incidentally a long viaduct, the crew of "Jinty" No. 47267 take a breather as their charge blows off impatiently prior to departure for Longsight. The picture is taken alongside the erstwhile grain warehouse which stood between Boad Street and Store Street on the stations north-west flank. Housing a bonded store and wine cellar, it once again reflected the variety and depth of GCR goods operations in the Manchester area. Ducie Street was eventually closed on 2nd October 1967 and the site extensively re-developed to form a station car park and a multi-storey office, Rail House, for British Rail.
Photo: B. K. B. Green

London & North Western Ry.
Issued subject to the conditions & regulations in the Cos Time Tables Books Bills & Notices & unless stated therein to be so NOT available by Irish Mail.
MANCHESTER (LONDON ROAD) TO
LONGSIGHT
(F)
THIRD CLASS] 372(S.) [Parly
LONGSIGHT FARE -/2
JE28.97
6805

34. London Road, 4th April 1957. Evidence of British Railways modernization plan is seen here in the form of a recently introducted "Derby Lightweight" dmu entering the eastern side of the station beneath the massive gantry carrying No. 2 signal box. Commissioned in 1909, the box had a frame of 143 levers and controlled signalling equipment and points utilizing the Webb/Thompson electric system as distinct from the pneumatic arrangement of the neighbouring GCR. Identification of the former LNWR boxes is made easier by the fact that the company numbered its signal boxes from the "London" end towards the relevant station. Astride the structure is a steel framed concrete "umbrella" added as a safety precaution against air raid attack of the Second World War. This fortification is reputed to have weighed no less than fifty tons. The signal box was one of no less than four in the area that were replaced during the weekend of the 23rd-25th April 1960 by the new London Road Power Box. The four were London Road Nos 1, 2 and 3 and Ardwick Junction. The former GC box had closed on 3rd February 1960.

Photo: B. K. B. Green

35. (Centre) London Road, 3rd September 1953. Enthusiasts unfamiliar with train workings in the Manchester area during this period may be taken aback by the appearance of this Class A3 Pacific locomotive No. 60107 *Royal Lancer* entering the station with a Marylebone express. At the time these magnificent machines were deployed on these particular workings over Woodhead. Due in at 3.29p.m., the train had left London at ten o'clock in the morning with stops at Leicester and Nottingham acting as a reminder that these two East Midland cities once had the luxury of a *choice* of direct services to Manchester.

The sprouting steelwork for overhead equipment on the eastern approaches to the station signals the imminent electrification of the Manchester, Sheffield and Wath route. Local services from Glossop and Hadfield commenced on the 14th June 1954 although Woodhead Tunnel had been opened some eleven days earlier enabling through electric working as far as Penistone. The first stage, energised in February 1952 enabled freight operation over the Wath, Penistone and Dunford Bridge sections. Stage three, between Penistone and Sheffield, was inaugurated on 20th September.

Photo: B. K. B. Green

36. London Road. A Carlisle (Kingmoor-12A) "Duchess" No. 46255 *City of Hereford* has her tank topped up by the crew prior to edging on to the turntable below No. 2 signal box. For reasons which are obscure, Longsight shed never possessed a turntable longer than 60′ which posed a distinct problem when turning an engine with a total wheelbase of 62′-11″! When the station turntable was removed, visiting Pacifics had to run out to Stockport to be turned on the triangle formed by the connecting lines east and west of Edgeley Junction — at Cheadle Village and Davenport junctions.

Photo: R. E. Gee

7. London Road, 2nd April 1957. The day nay not be that far away when still photographs will be able to record sound s well as the action. Unfortunately, such possibilities were undreamed of when Brian Green caught Royal Scot Class No. 46160 *Queen Victoria's Rifleman* ndulging in what must have been a truly hunderous bout of slipping as she pulled ut of London Road on a showery April ay with the 2.0p.m. to Euston.

Photo: B. K. B. Green

8. (Centre) London Road, 2nd June 1954. Until modernization and rebuilding, London Road had effectively been two tations in one. From the early beginnings n 1840 and the "temporary" station in Travis Street, the station had been a joint ffair with each company maintaining its own offices, staff and booking arrangements. This position had been consolidated with the passing of the London Road Station Act of 1859 which compelled the MS&L and LNWR to put their ffairs in order. Platforms were partitioned between the resultant railways, asting at least until 1959 and a Station Superintendent was appointed to keep natters under control. Almost one hundred years on, this view south shows eatures that made it possible to identify he territorial divisions along the pproach lines. The different semaphore ignals disclose their former owners eelings on design, the GC to the left possessing slender arms surmounted by piked finials.

On the left Class B1 4-6-0 No 61284 olls in with an express from Marylebone whilst a 2-6-4 tank engine on its way to Longsight is held at bay by the bold, broad, arms of the LNWR Signals. To the ight of the picture, beyond Temperence Street, is Mayfield Station, a separately named entity opened by the LNWR in 910 as an overflow to the ever busy main tation.

Photo: B. K. B. Green

9. London Road, February 1952. The last ection of railway from Stockport to Manchester is on a brick built viaduct which commences at Ardwick. Most of the structure dates from 1840 but has been widened to accommodate the dditional lines as required. The original alignment lies to the right of this view which shows Britannia class locomotive No. 70031 *Byron* approaching London Road with a short train of corridor stock on the down fast line. The parapet wall to he left of the picture runs parallel to North Western Street, relocated as a esult of plans to widen the viaduct in 905. At this point several sidings were aid to improve access to the goods depots behind London Road and to allow for the new station which became Mayfield. The wo lines to the left of the train were known as the up slow and up fast respectively until electrification when they became the up and down fast. The track o the right until latterly formed the Mayfield station headshunt. The massed chimneys and roof tops of Ardwick have ong since vanished and the corner shop at the junction of Union Street and Temperance Street is but a memory, having vanished beneath the Mancunian Way.

Photo: B. K. B. Green

40. Mayfield, 11th April 1954. Despite the completion in 1881 of considerable extension work, the LNWR found London Road unable to cope with their ever burgeoning requirements. Expansion was only available at an adjacent site and so Mayfield came into being on the opposite side of Fairfield Street. The new station, in traditional LNWR style, opened on 10th August 1910. No attempt had been made to emulate the spacious London Road itself, the company settling for a good solid functional structure in red engineering brick dressed with sandstone. A simple style of hipped transverse roofing covered the platforms. In this view it shows former GC/LNE 4-4-2T Class C13 No. 67407 awaiting departure with a stopping train to Hayfield. Mayfield incidentally received a direct hit by a landmine during a raid by the Luftwaffe on 22nd December 1940, an event vividly recalled by Harold Gorton, a retired senior Longsight driver who narrowly escaped death on the footplate of his "Cauliflower" by having departed only seconds before. *Photo: B. K. B. Green*

41. Mayfield, 1959. This view from the platform ends towards the junction with the main lines shows electrification work well advanced. Old signalling equipment stands defiantly amidst the changing scene as the remodelling moves towards its final stages. Mayfield had traditionally been controlled by London Road No. 1 signal box but the new Power Box, which would eventually control all movements in the area, would not be ready for some months. During the changeover, arrangements to enable Mayfield to function with some normality were made and included provision of a temporary signal box, seen here to the right, which was brought into use as a block post on the 25th April 1960. On completion of the main line remodelling the new London Road Power Box assumed control of Mayfield, allowing the temporary box to be closed, all points being converted to hand operation, passenger traffic ceasing after a period of over fifty years. The station continued in use as a parcels concentration depot until withdrawal of traffic by Royal Mail in 1986 ultimately forced closure. *Photo: G. H. Platt*

42. Mayfield, 1959. Another view of the signalling equipment installed by the LNWR shows this fine array of bracketed signals mounted on lattice girders which formerly supported sections of the roof. The six signals shown here controlled departures from the station's four platforms. That to the left was starter for platform 1 and when "off" indicated the route clear on to the up slow line. The inner pairs controlled platforms 2 and 3 but in this instance allowed access to either up slow or up fast lines.

Photo: G. H. Platt

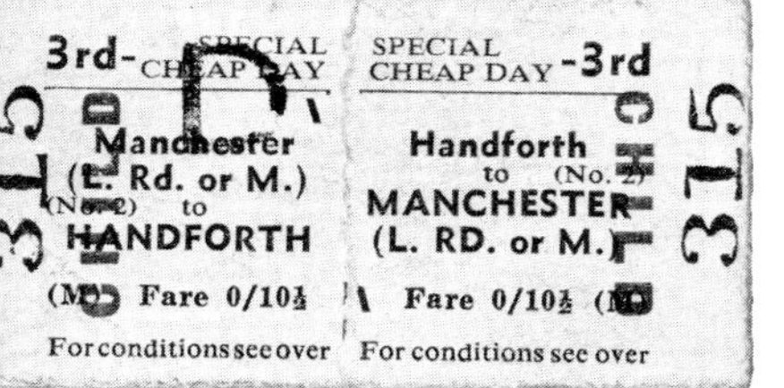

43. London Road, 2nd September 1958. A ground-level view across the abandoned turntable well as the site is prepared for the forthcoming modernization. Closure of the railway between here and Oxford Road was required to remodel the rail approaches and build the new bridge and platforms over Fairfield Street. The new London Road Power Signal Box was to be built on the left of the site vacated by the turntable and the up and down slow lines serving platforms 13 and 14 would appear in a position approximately where the truncated track approached the turntable. The footbridge to Mayfield is on the left. The signal to the right with its associated calling-on arm is wire-operated from the MSJ&A box situated beyond the footbridge, a distinction being that other signals at the station were electrically operated as mentioned previously. *Photo: R. E. Gee*

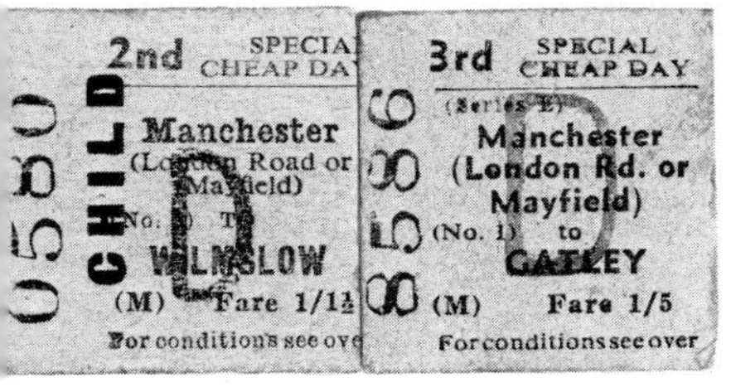

44. London Road, 20th March 1957. Moving away from the MSJ&A platform at London Road with the stock of the 9.27a.m. arrival from Ditton Junction (dep 8.13) via Warrington and Lymm is Ivatt 2-6-2 tank No. 41210. It was usual for the carriages to be shunted into the main station before being taken to Longsight for servicing. The stock returned later to form the 12.25p.m. to Ditton Junction, stopping along the way at Oxford Road, Sale, Timperley, Broadheath, Dunham Massey, Heatley and Warburton, Lymm, Latchford, Warrington Arpley, Warrington Bank Quay L. L., and Widnes. In the background, businessmen settle in comfort for the departure of "The Mancunian" at 9.35a.m.

Photo: B. K. B. Green

45. (Above) London Road, 9th September 1958. The impressive outlines of one of Manchester's premier seats of learning, the John Dalton building of the University of Manchester Institute of Science and Technology (UMIST) stands high above the MSJ&A line as it approaches London Road. This is the so called "South Junction" section of line, carried for its entire length on a viaduct, built for the opening of the railway in 1849. A train of empty coaching stock, probably from Cornbrook carriage sidings, enters London Road station hauled bunker first by Fowler 2-6-4 tank No. 42354. At this point the MSJ&A line diverges to run either side of what is ostensibly an island platform. The tracks to the left reached a dead end formerly served by a turntable until the advent of electric traction on the Altrincham line which did not require turning. *Photo: R. E. Gee*

47. (Below) London Road, 9th September 1958. The South Junction side of the station showing the signal box and the trainshed wall, completed in 1882 with the extension of the station. An unidentified Stanier 2-6-4 tank locomotive stands on the "through road" waiting for a path to Longsight with the pilot goods trip from Ordsall Lane. The girders of the bridge on which the train is standing were removed in 1959 as part of the scheme to reconstruct London Road Station. The two wrought iron bridges were replaced by a single prestressed concrete span cantilevered to take track, either side of the island platform. This reconstruction represented one of the biggest single civil engineering tasks undertaken in the rebuilding and modernization programme. Behind the signal box can be seen the lattice girders of the footbridge connecting the MSJ&A platforms — rebuilt in 1882 — with the rest of the station. To the right is the footbridge to Mayfield, a reminder to many of the impromptu energetic walk required on the realization that it — Mayfield — was something of a distance away from the main station. *Photo: R. E. Gee*

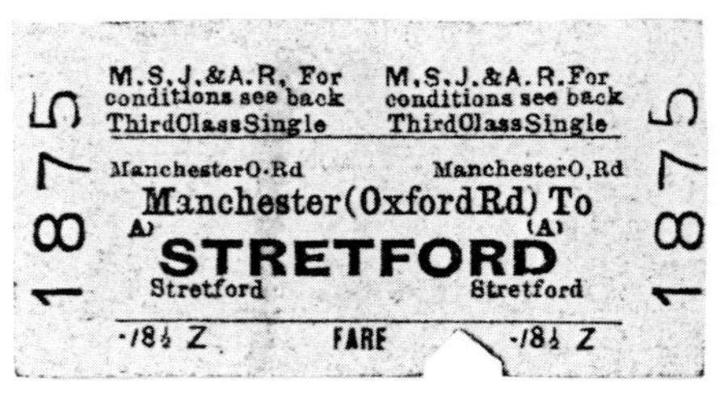

48. (Right, opposite page) Oxford Road, 9th September 1959. The burnished buffers of MSJ&A Unit No. M28577M almost precede the arrival of the train as it rounds the curve over Oxford Road bridge and into the station after its short trip from London Road. This most intensive service had a weekday service of sixty or so trains for the twenty two minute journey with as many as ten trains leaving Altrincham between eight and nine o'clock in the morning. The station is in the throes of modernization, only a few days before a complete shutdown of the section to London Road. *Photo: R. E. Gee*

46. (Above) London Road, 9th September 1958. T MSJ&A side of London Road had its own signal bo a 30 lever structure at the Oxford Road end of t "island" platform. Students of signal box design w notice the overhang of the timber upper sectic necessitated by structure gauge requirements. (standard LNWR design to size "E" (18'-9" length), the box dated from 1915 replacing a Saxt and Farmer structure of 1877. As with most MSJ& signal boxes, contractors' lever frames were used, th particular one being to the design of the Railwa Signalling Company. The close proximity of t sliding windows to the overhead contact wire will noticed and current safety regulations now requi the windows to be screened over with a mesh guar Notice also the shorter than usual arm of the uppe quadrant semaphore signal, a characteristic of th line. Temporary closure between Oxford Road ar London Road, to allow for rebuilding, from 15 September 1958, resulted in abolition of this box ar subsequent demolition. *Photo: R. E. G*

49. (centre) Oxford Road, 25th January 1955. Compared to the city's other stations, there was a distinct "down-town" flavour about Oxford Road, although no doubt the timber buildings were very robustly constructed. Memories will no doubt be evoked by the sight of the Morris "Traveller" to be seen here flouting the parking regulations. A solitary electric light can be seen inside the ground floor of the building attempting to illuminate what appears to be a very gloomy interior. To the left an advertisement offers a cheap trip to Huddersfield for a football match. The fare of four shillings (20p) could be claimed to be a travel bargain. *Photo: British Rail*

50. (Bottom) Oxford Road, May 1931. The station at Oxford Road provided terminal facilities for MSJ&A trains, the two platforms adjacent to Gloucester Street — now Whitworth Street West — proving adequate for the line's needs. Local trains, having been tried unsuccessfully in 1857 began to work through to London Road in 1878 and ultimately nearly all services on the Altrincham line started and finished there. This view towards Knott Mill from the island platform shows the through or "back" line from London Road coming in on the left. Fowler 2-6-2 tank No. 15507 stands alongside platform four, one of the two terminal platforms previously mentioned, with trains bound for Altrincham shortly before the introduction of the electric service. Of interest is the "MSJ&A" legend on the coach, an LNWR style panelled brake third built for the line at Wolverton in 1911. Both upper and lower quadrant types of signal are on view, the former, to the left, having shortened arms. The fully electrified service over the MSJ&A began on 11th May 1931.
Photo: G. H. Platt

51. Oxford Road, 9th September 1958. A panoramic view of the station from the signal box. The original terminal platforms to the left have been closed to passenger traffic to allow for reconstruction. Oxford Road had been rebuilt on previous occasions, in 1903, and had also sustained air raid damage in the blitz of December 1940 (*of* sections on Castlefield viaduct and Exchange Station). Though we tend to think of the station as one for short and medium haul passenger trains it is worth mentioning the service to London operated from here by the LNWR. The "Bradshaw" timetable for 1922 shows a morning departure for the Capital (Saturdays excepted) at 10.30a.m. with conditional stops at MSJ&A stations, Hale, Mobberley and also Knutsford. Travelling then via Middlewich and Sandbach, Crewe was reached at 11.50 — where a luncheon car was attached — and Euston at 3.10p.m. A down train left London at 2.30p.m. — teas being served between here and Crewe — and arrived at Oxford Road at 7.08. Unlike the morning train, the down service connected with London Road, arrival being four minutes later. Another notable Oxford Road departure was the Llandudno "Club" train which used the station when Exchange was out of commission after the ravages of December 1940. *Photo: R. E. Gee*

52. Knott Mill and Deansgate, 13th May 1965. Leaving Oxford Road, the station at Knott Mill is quickly encountered before the lines part at Castlefield Junction, Cornbrook to the left and Ordsall Lane to the right. Nowadays abbreviated to simply *Deansgate*, the station does a brisk trade in commuter traffic with the added attraction of Freightliner trains to and from the depot at Trafford Park for the enthusiast. In recent times, the opening of the "G-Mex" centre on the adjacent Central Station site has given an additional fillip to traffic, the station having been connected by a specially designed bridge over Whitworth Street West. The station was rebuilt considerably towards the end of the nineteenth century, taking basically the form shown in this view towards Castlefield Junction. The overhead equipment did not of course appear until 1930 and the canopy to the right has been removed along with the "Gentlemen" facility to the left. *Photo: P. E. Baughan*

53. Castlefield, c. 1967. A three car "Altrincham" set makes its way along the MSJ&A viaduct alongside the Bridgewater Canal, having just negotiated Castlefield Junction signal box to the right of the timber yard crane. This view from Egerton Street also shows the approach lines to Central Station, on the far right, behind the 1849 brick structure. The original line into Central ran alongside the MSJ&A viaduct albeit at a higher level, and was part of an overall scheme sanctioned by the Cheshire Lines Act of 22nd July 1872. The joint engineers for the approach line to the station from Cornbrook Junction were Sacré, Johnson and A. Johnstone (Midland Engineer) and H. L. Moorsom was resident engineer for the station works. The design was detailed to include castellations, included to appease the conservationists of the period who objected to the destruction of the Roman Fort site. The high level girders which crossed the Bridgewater Navigation were constructed by Messrs Eastwood Swingler & Co of Derby. The spans of the openings were 203 feet and 145 feet respectively, costing £16,693. The line was formerly opened on 26th June 1877 and to the public on 9th July. Additional traffic and construction by the Great Northern Railway of a warehouse and offices on Deansgate required the widening of the viaduct to take four tracks. This was carried out on the north side and once again required extensive bridgeworks over the water section, and opening in 1898. *Photo: J. Clark (courtesy G. M. Museum)*

54. Castlefield, 17th June 1942. This view shows the south side of the MSJ&A line between Cornbrook East and Castlefield junctions. The purpose of the photograph was to record the re-constructed MSJ&A viaduct, destroyed here during the blitz on Manchester between December 21st-23rd 1940. Whilst the line was out of use MSJ&A trains terminated at Warwick Road where there were four tracks. A steam-hauled shuttle service was run into Central lasting until September 21st 1941 by which time the new viaduct was ready for use. Visible in the background is the viaduct carrying the CLC lines up and along into Central which fortunately had escaped damage. Below is an arm of the Bridgewater Canal connecting the River Irwell to the wharves at Castlefield. Situated in Manchester's Hulme district, these various canal arms and wharves presented a somewhat seedy view of the city to the incoming rail traveller. In recent years, the canal has been cleaned up and the Castlefield area, with its Roman connections, is being promoted as a tourist attraction. Trains have not run along the viaduct into Central since the latter's closure in 1969, although under plans for Manchester's LRT system it could be used again to bring the 'Supertrams' along from G-Mex to connect with the Altrincham line. *Photo: Authors Collection*

55. (Above) Manchester Central, 10th June 1953. The view across Windmill Street with decorations for Queen Elizabeth II's Coronation still very much in evidence. Although this was high summer, hats and long coats were still in vogue.
Photo: British Rail

56. (Right) Midland Hotel, 13th May 1965. In contrast to an earlier picture we have a rear view of the Midland Hotel, its towering splendour dominating the scene from the south east side of Lower Mosley Street. *Photo: P. E. Baughan*

57. (Below) Midland Hotel, 13th May 1965. At the rear of the hotel is this superb terracotta moulding over the doorway that at one time was a direct entrance from the forecourt of Central Station. The Midland "Wyvern" and coat of arms are flanked by two cherubs and although such Baroque style floridity may not be to everyone's taste, one can only marvel at the craftsmanship that produced it. *Photo: P. E. Baughan*

Exchange

Manchester Exchange, Station Approach, March,1928: The broad, cobbled roadway has a characteristic dampness to it as we lookacross to the massive Exchange train shed with part of the Italianate frontage visible over on the right-hand side. Railway premises appear to have attracted advertising material almost from their inception and Exchange in this era was no exception. The LMS themselves are offering 2900 square feet of freehold property in the vicinity of the station. Gross rentals will total £1768 per annum (!) H.Samuel's watches (the company is still with us today) are advertised next to Messrs.Parry whose furniture is available from their premises on Downing Street-where the Mancunian Way flyover is today. Jewsbury & Brown's Dry Ginger Ale, along with Crossley Oil Engines-both from Manchester-based concerns, are offered to passers-by. The ubiquitous Bovril advertisements nestle below the LMS hoarding which proclaims travel delights on offer from the company: cheap return tickets to Bolton ("every train, every day"), Leeds and Blackpool, Rhyl, Colwyn Bay and Llandudno are set to tempt the Easter Weekend traveller for 5/-. Matlock-"served by the LMS main line" (alas, no more), vies for business with Dunkerque, Paris and Brussels. Remember, though, these were hard times and five shillings was an awful lot of money to someone earning only £2-£3 a week! The Daily Dispatch, one of the Kemsley group's newspapers, is flaunted on a neon sign above the train shed. The paper was printed in Withy Grove, just across from the station. In those days Exchange, and neighbouring Victoria, would be bustling with newspaper traffic-a source of revenue now all but lost to today's rail network. *H.W. Bennett ¢ National Railway Museum.*

Manchester Exchange, August 1961: Giving a good view of the interior of the train shed, Stanier 2-6-4 Tank No.**42610** barks vigorously away along the through road between platforms 3 and 4 whilst engaged in a shunting manoeuvre with a fitted box van. A Metro-Cammell DMU waits alongside platform 3-the extension of No. 11 from Victoria which created the famous 2,235 ft.long platform. The rump of the bombed-out wall of the once-splendid Italianate frontage is just visible above the DMU.
E.M.Johnson.

Manchester Exchange, February 28th.1953: A last look at the well-remembered west end, a scene frequented by scores of "Spotters", photographers and observers of all ages over the years. Black 5 No.**45074**, a Crewe South engine, lifts a train of empty coaching stock away from platform 3. The tall chimney and water tower in the left background belong to Messrs.Threlfalls situated in the Strangeways district. A distinctive aroma emanating from these premises has lent a certain "something" to this area over the years, leaving visitors in no doubt as to their whereabouts!
Tom Lewis.

Manchester Exchange, n.d: The west-facing aspect of Exchange yielded three semi-circular, glass-fronted gables. Thus identified, this has caused the station to be variously confused with Manchester London Road and Liverpool Lime Street in assorted railway books! Here, though, we need be in no doubt about our whereabouts as we watch "Patriot" No.**45507** *Royal Tank Corps* pull sharply away from platform 3 with a Manchester-Barrow express.
W.D.Cooper.

Victoria

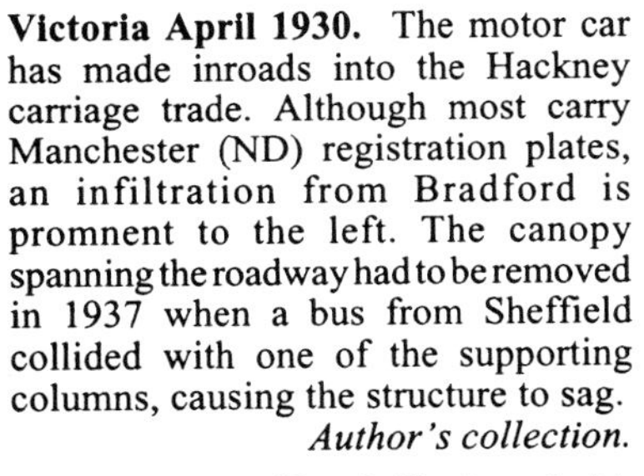

Victoria April 1930. The motor car has made inroads into the Hackney carriage trade. Although most carry Manchester (ND) registration plates, an infiltration from Bradford is promnent to the left. The canopy spanning the roadway had to be removed in 1937 when a bus from Sheffield collided with one of the supporting columns, causing the structure to sag. *Author's collection.*

Looking Along Hunt's Bank, n.d: At 2.53 precisely, the smoke-blackened facade of the Dawes extension, completed in 1909 after eight year's work, faces the camera. On the left is the frontage of the original Victoria of 1844. Across Hunt's Bank is the rather severe-looking offices of the Lancashire and Yorkshire Railway. The motor car, undreamed of in young Victoria's day, would still have been something of a rare bird when the 1901building work was finished. Today, its all-pervading presence manifests itself in the shape of machines that look almost as strange as some of the early locomotives that once barked their way along behind those grand slabs of stone. *Author's collection.*

Victoria. April 1930. The year 1992 saw a commencement of work to create a large sports complex on much of the site covered by platforms 12 to 16. Piecemeal removal of the overall roof had covered a period of more than sixty years, commencing in 1929 with works to form the longest platform in Europe. The linking of platform 11 (Victoria) and 3 (Exchange) created a 2,235 feet long platform which can be seen to the left of this view. The overall plan included for the resignalling of both stations and the four pictures reproduced on this and the adjoining page illustrate some of the changes that occurred. The view above is along platform 11 looking west, the new signalling in place. Beyond the roof, the outline of one of the new signal boxes can just be established, Victoria West Junction. The view of this box is reproduced below. *H.W. Bennett.*

Victoria. April 1930. View looking north from platform 11 towards platform 12. Much of this area was affected by the bomb damage of 1940 and the "temporary" nature of the repairs was never made fully to look more than just that. The advertising hoardings clearly devote much of the available space to the virtues of visiting the northern resorts of the LMS empire. *H.W. Bennett.*

Victoria. Late 1927. One of the signal boxes rendered extinct by the scheme was this structure seen here, sited beneath the overall roof at the north end of the station. *H.W. Bennett.*

Victoria East Junction, July 1931: At East Junction two pairs of lines turned sharply into the station complex. This was the Manchester Loop Line-a relief route opened in 1878 from here to Thorp's Bridge Junction, Newton Heath. Controlling the traffic here was Victoria East Junction signalbox, a Lancashire and Yorkshire Railway affair and complete with a splendid array of that company's semaphores; all, be it noted, wire-operated. Appearing under the gantry is "Crab" 2-6-0 No.**13028** at the head of an excursion from St.Pancras-awakening memories of Midland Railway running powers through the station from Ashbury's via Midland Junction, Phillips Park and Miles Platting. The coaching stock is of the late LNWR 57 ft. variety; most of it looks still to be still in the company's "plum and off-white" livery. *E.R.Morten.*

Victoria Station, through lines, June 15th.1961: "Jubilee" No.**45663** *Jervis* heads along the Up Main line with an express for Yorkshire. Bound out of neighbouring Exchange Station, the engine looks all ready for the assault on the Miles Platting Bank (Hunt's Bank Incline). Victoria was always a confusing mixture of line designations: at Victoria East Junction the Up and Down lines became reversed - *Jervis* will pass shortly onto the Down Slow and then Down Fast line on the first leg of its journey eastwards. *Gordon Coltas.*

Victoria Station, Platform 11, looking east, n.d: This year, 1993, has seen the demise of a once-great station. In this picture the remains of the now-demolished fine overall roof spanning platforms 12-16 dominate the scene as "Jubilee" No.**45705** *Seahorse* treads cautiously across from platform 11 with a stopping passenger working. The train is heading towards Victoria West Junction prior to taking the Down Slow line in the direction of Salford. *A.H.Bryant.*

London Road

London Road, c.1920: The smoke-blackened train shed roof dwarfs the bulk of LNWR "Claughton" No.**1914**. Named *PATRIOT* and sub-titled: *IN MEMORY OF THE FALLEN L&NWR EMPLOYEES 1914 TO 1919* this, the LNWR's War Memorial engine, has arrived with a stopping passenger train. By the looks of things, the train has come in alongside platform 4 (the current platform 9). The twin columns supporting the roof identify the joining of the 1866 station and the later, 1882, extension. The presence of two official-looking gentlemen and a police officer suggests something special, possibly an Armistice Day working.

Author's collection.

Manchester London Road, n.d: A view from the footbridge that spanned the east end of the station. London Road Station comprised essentially four parts as far as passenger workings were concerned: 1) The Great Central section consisting of three platforms lettered 'A' 'B' and 'C' to avoid confusion with those of the LNWR. 2) The LNWR platforms-six all told and numbered, rather confusingly, 1-7. 3) The Up and Down MSJ&A platforms carrying the local services to and from Altrincham and (inter alia) those to Liverpool and Warrington over the Lymm line via Timperley and Broadheath junctions. 4) Mayfield, effectively an "overflow" station from London Road and housing four platforms on the south side of Fairfield Street in a rather plain-looking red brick building. Our footbridge view looks along the train shed towards the booking offices. At platform 1 an LNWR 4-4-0, one of the company's celebrated "Precursors", awaits departure with an express; blower on and safety valves lifting, columns of shimmering power vaporising in the glare beneath the vastness of the train shed roof-75 feet across between the supporting pillars. Notice the iron railings forming a rigid boundary between the rival companies. Evidence of London Road's "two company" status prevailed until modern times.

British Rail.

Manchester London Road, August 27th.1953: The London Road of the 1950s-as known by myself and countless other young enthusiasts of the time. This is 1953, Coronation year-a memorable one for Britons young and old alike; young Queen Elizabeth II is newly-crowned as we survey a scene packed with activity. Standing on the footbridge we are looking towards Ardwick amidst a thicket of semaphores, notice the slender arms belonging to the former Great Central; how these contrast with the short, stubby electrically-operated semaphores of LNWR parentage! Waiting to depart from platform 4 with an Up express is "Royal Scot" No.**46155** *The Lancer*. Its work over, Longsight (9A) Caprotti "Black 5" No.**44687** barks

away from platform 7 and heads off back to base. Below, perched on the railings are several young "spotters". This is a Thursday, still plenty time in the school holidays to perhaps catch another "namer" or two. Over on the former Great Central side of the station, the masts and supports for the long-awaited Manchester-Sheffield electrification scheme are in place. In front of the ex-G.C. signalbox, workmen are busy erecting a necessary extension to the box, soon electric traction will begin to glide in and out of here. Less than another decade later and London Road will be "all-electric"-a changed place indeed. *Gordon Coltas.*

Manchester London Road, Summer, 1960: Beginning in 1958, London Road station became immersed in the turmoil of rebuilding. The facade, offices and booking hall, designed by Mills and Murgatroyd and dating back to 1866, were swept away. In their place rose the glass and concrete edifice that became "Piccadilly." Much detail is visible in this splendid panorama taken from the roof of the former London Road Fire Station on the corner of Fairfield Street. The station approach, rising from the junction of London Road/Ducie Street and Auburn Street is thronged with cars and passengers-a busy time for London Road, it is five-past ten in the morning. In the centre of the roadway, as today, taxi cabs await their fares. Looking down towards Piccadilly, both Manchester and Salford Corporation buses -the old 95 and 96 routes-figure prominently anmongst the traffic, London Road was busy even then. Shades of pre-Grouping ownership are still manifest: the three gables of the former LNWR's goods warehouse stand out prominently at the base of the approach; alongside, lorries and trailers await the arrival of goods; a considerable quantity of goods vans are marshalled and can be seen projecting out from under the canopy. Along Ducie Street the Great Central's "London" goods warehouse dominates the scene, and happily survives yet to tell the tale. Bearing round towards the passenger side of the station, the grain warehouse, once the property of the Great Central, can be seen. In front of this is the temporary wooden booking office that did duty until the new station opened for business. The right-hand side of the old station frontage has gone, in its place has risen the steelwork of the new building; high above the roar of the traffic and the sound of escaping steam and dotted around the spidery framework, men with a head for heights clamber over the steel sinews. The Italianate towers of the old Fire Station show as a pleasing architectural touch. In the lower foreground can be seen the firemens' quarters; whole families lived in this once-busy complex which housed not only a large working fire station, but a bank and a Coroner's court. London Road, to be certain, as it will never be seen again.

British Rail.

Manchester London Road, MSJ&A platforms, April 29th.1958: Features of a bygone era show in this view, taken just prior to the onset of the modernisation and rebuilding of the station. No less than six signalboxes were required to control traffic in and out of London Road and its environs. One such was London Road MSJ&A-built to an LNWR standard design (size "E" with a Railway Signal Company frame with 30 levers) and possessing an overhang front and back to clear the running lines. This side of London Road saw sweeping changes upon rebuilding-in particular the construction of a long island platform (numbered 13 and 14) which projected over the Fairfield Street bridge in the foreground. Notice the lengthy footbridge in the background. Some 45 yards long, this also spanned Fairfield Street and connected Mayfield Station with the other parts of the London Road complex.

British Railways.

Approaches to Manchester London Road, April 3rd.1957: Railway writing down the years has almost always tended to concentrate on passenger workings. Doubtless, the glamour and romance associated with named engines and travel-especially of the long-distance variety-coupled with the fact that much freight travelled at night, was responsible for this attitude. To parallel this, goods yards tended to be out of bounds to most enthusiasts, and plates and film were often both scarce and expensive. In consequence, the prima donnas of the railway world more often than not took centre stage. Though we looked at freight workings over the MSJ&A lines in a previous picture, these were the tip of the iceberg as far as London Road was concerned. Both the LNWR and the GC had very big freight interests here. Access to these was via independent sets of goods lines-two for each company. Here, an immaculate BR Standard 2-10-0, No.**92127**, heads a through freight over the goods lines of the former LNWR and along towards the warehouse down at street-level.
B.K.B.Green.

Manchester London Road, May 13th.1958: In this view, we extend our horizons and look at the freight scene nearer towards the station. The photographer is stood in front of the parapet wall which overlooked North Western Street. Immediately adjacent are the two former Great Central goods lines-notice the GC lower-quadrant semaphore still extant at this late date; behind, are the goods lines of the former LNWR. Overhead is the 1500v DC catenary of the Manchester-Sheffield-Wath scheme, soon that of the later 25 kv AC Manchester-Crewe scheme will adjoin. All the goods lines ran down to street-level to an area bounded by Travis Street, Sheffield Street and Ducie Street. Here, the warehouses and yards lay. Of interest are the tarpaulined wagons, a hangover from early days and only superceded in modern times. The two-storey building projecting from the ex GC side of the train shed, housed an oil store and lamp room.
British Railways.

Manchester Oxford Road, June 21st.1961: A newly rebuilt Oxford Road station-an official view taken from platform 2 looking towards Manchester Piccadilly. The tower of the Refuge building on the corner of Oxford Road and Whitworth Street dominates the scene and dwarfs the famous "Armadillo" paltform canopies. Of laminated timber construction, these caused something of a stir when the station re-opened. Over on platform 4 an MSJ&A 1500 v dc EMU (**M28579M**) awaits departure for Altrincham. On the through lines the catenary is alive at 25kv enabling the Class 304 EMUs to operate from here to Crewe; another ten years were to elapse before through running was achieved, using this voltage, to Altrincham. *British Railways.*

Oxford Road

Manchester Oxford Road, March 11th.1967: A close-up of one of the now-celebrated and quite-lamented LMS 1500v dc EMUS-**M29241** - forming the 12.10 pm train to Altrincham. Built for the opening of through electric services between Altrincham and London Road in 1931, these units became something of a legend and contributed in no small way to the pun "many short journeys and absolute reliability" (MSJ&A). It is worth mentioning that the MSJ&A trains, dating from May 28th.1849, have now entered their fourth phase. The advent of "Metrolink" has enabled through running from Altrincham via Manchester city centre to Bury.
Gordon Coltas.

Manchester Oxford Road, n.d: Prior to re-electrification at 25 kv in 1971, signalling over the Altrincham line had been by traditional block working. The signalling equipment on the MSJ&A was something of a mixture: LNWR, GCR, Railway Signal Company and Saxby and Farmer all being involved along the line at vartious points in history. Unlike its neighbour at London Road, the signalbox at Oxford Road was of Great Central design and dated from 1897. Formerly "Oxford Road West" this was one of two boxes once sited here. The other, designated "Oxford Road East", was an overhead structure of MS&L parentage. It was demolished in March 1931 in advance of the electrification which came onstream the following month. Some MSJ&A signalling equipment lasted an awful long time: Altrincham North box, closed and demolished in the summer of 1991 had LNWR single-needle block instruments right to the end. *G.H.Platt.*

Manchester Oxford Road, June 16th.1960: The interior of Oxford Road signalbox showing clearly the 40-lever Railway Signal Company frame and new power panel. To the right can be seen the train describer covering movements between here and Piccadilly (note that the power box and signals controlled by the latter were referred to as "LR" -London Road). The signalman is operating a route-setting switch at the bottom of the panel. This OCS operation ("one control switch") was based on the "NX" ("entrance and exit") system first used at Brunswick, on the Cheshire Lines, in 1937. Off to the right is a standard BR block instrument controlling operations between Oxford Road and Castlefield Junction. A strange combination of old and new technology is seen here: the ensemble lasted until the Central Station closure programme was enacted in May, 1969. Re-signalling of the MSJ&A line was undertaken-part of a £225,000 programme; the box at Oxford Road disappeared, with control of the line now under the auspices of the London Road power box as far as Deansgate Junction. *British Railways.*

Manchester Central, n.d: This is the sight that greeted photographer P.F.Cooke when he visited the station in the early years of the century: standing between platforms 5 and 6 an immaculately-groomed Midland Railway 2-4-0 locomotive-No.**142** of the 1070 Class. No.142 was built by Sharp Stewart to a design by Kirtley and was rebuilt to the form seen here by S.W.Johnson. With 6'-2½" coupled wheels, these splendid little engines lacked something of the grace inherent in the larger Midland 4-coupled classes, but possessed, nevertheless, all the hallmarks of Johnson's finesse; this despite the application of the Deeley chimney and smokebox door. Notice the engine retains the curved handrail-a small Johnsonian subtlety. Alongside platform 4, underneath the light and dark brown striped platform awnings, a characteristic of the CLC, Compound No.**1021**, one of the 1906 engines, awaits departure. *P.F.Cooke*

Manchester Central, n.d: More vintage Midland at Central. R.M.Deeley's large and powerful 0-6-4 suburban tank engines were quite unlike anything seen before in Midland circles. Together with David Bain's close-coupled and arc-roofed bogie carriages, the "Block" or "Woofle" tanks as they were variously called, caused something of a revolution in suburban working both here in Manchester and elsewhere. No.**2000**, the pioneer of forty engines in the class all built at Derby in 1907, waits to leave Central with an Up suburban train over the South District line. The picture can be dated as prior to 1920; from that point the Deeley tanks were rebuilt with superheated boilers and Belpaire fireboxes. *Author's collection.*

Central

Manchester Central, c.1899: A rare view of an MS&L engine, which, though carrying the Great Central insignia, is still in almost original condition. Class 3 2-4-2 tank engine No.**592** was built by Neilsons in October 1890 to a design by Thomas Parker. Of particular note are the stovepipe chimney, drip-feed lubricator and polished tyres. Notice, too, the large engine head lamps displaying a local code; these engines are known to have worked stopping passenger services over the Fallowfield line to Guide Bridge. Worth a second glance are the Cheshire Lines semaphores with their rather peculiar inward-mounted spectacles. *Collection of W.G.Rear.*

Manchester Central, late 1930s: Once the pride and joy of the Great Central, former Class 1 (LNER B2) No.**5427** *City of London* moves away from platform 8 with a local train, bound, almost certainly, over the Fallowfield line for Guide Bridge. Notice the new signalbox standing overhead in the background, commissioned in 1935, and the straight-cut awnings over the platforms. The engine is in LNER green lined out in black and white. The first coach of the local is a former MS&L brake third with a guard's ducket. *W.Potter.*

Manchester Central, 1948: Original Great Central "Director" 4-4-0 No.**2655** *The Earl of Kerry* pulls away from platform 9 with a stopping train to Chester. These classic 4-4-0s had been in evidence at Central from their inception before the First War. Some of the later post-War engines (Class 11F-LNER D11) were a common sight on station pilot duty in the mid to late 1950s. Grubby and run-down, the elderly "Directors" gave a touch of aristocracy and provided a marked contrast to Stanier's Black 5s and Jubilees that were so much the staple diet of those far-off days. *H.C.Casserley.*

Manchester Central, n.d: In complete contrast to our previous views we look to more modern times and the sight of Diesel power alongside platform 2 in the shape of Type 2 Bo-Bo No.D5015. Later designated Class 24, these 1,160 hp Diesel-electric engines had been introduced to the BR system in 1958. A press release from British Railways (East Lancashire Division) dated Friday, September 19th.that year reports that: "......built at Derby works earlier this year has been running on test pulling the 9.38.a.m. Derby to Manchester train, arriving at Manchester Central at 11.20 a.m. The locomotive has then worked the 12.30 p.m. Manchester Central to Liverpool Central train , and this is the first occasion that a Diesel-electric main line locomotive has been seen on this section of line." **D5015** is probably waiting to depart with the 11.20 Liverpool train; in complete contrast, 4F No.**44088** waits alongside in the loco release road.

A.H.Bryant.

0039

British Railways Board (M)
The Locomotive Club of Great Britain
(North West Branch)
The Manchester Terminals Farewell
Rail Tour
SATURDAY 3rd MAY 1969
Manchester (Exchange) Depart 10.30 hrs. to
MANCHESTER (CENTRAL)
via various associated routes
SECOND CLASS For conditions see over

0039

Manchester Central, Saturday May 3rd.1969: The impressive single-span roof seen on the last full day of operation. Only DMUs forming services to Liverpool Central are seen in this rather wistful view. A lone figure, complete with rucksack, stands on platform 6; through the archway off to the right is platform 8 the sight of which forever evokes fond memories of trips home to Didsbury. Though viewed now as the GMEX Centre I'm sure no railway enthusiast of my generation will ever think of this building as anything else than "Central". *G.K.Fox.*

58. Central, 2nd May 1969. Compared to the other Manchester termini, Central had no sweeping approach or grand facade. Walking out of the station, the traveller was confronted by a shallow cobbled slope, although this view was relieved by the sight of the very impressive Midland Hotel. The roadway here continued through to run between platforms 2 and 3 being used by the ubiquitous mail and parcel vans. Across Windmill Street, the rather drab-looking building once housed the offices of Messrs. Simon Carves which later became Henry Simon Ltd., an engineering concern of world-wide repute. The lady with the umbrella provides proof of Manchester's moist climate; although, contrary to popular belief, the city has several dry days each year!

Photo: M. S. Welch

59. Central, 2nd May 1969. The platform concourse in its last hours, but there is nothing here to suggest a station in its death throes. After closure and lifting of track, the building did duty as a car-park for a number of years and to those of us who had known it well, it was an eerie sight walking over this ground in later years, one half-expected to see a train or hear a hiss of steam or have your ears assailed by a station announcer! The ticket offices on the left were not intended to be permanent. Built out of wood, they were erected as a temporary measure, pending the building of a hotel at the front of the station, as at St. Pancras. The picture shows a remarkable number of candid poses, as well as providing an insight into the fashions of the nineteen sixties, do any readers recognise themselves?

Photo: M. S. Welch

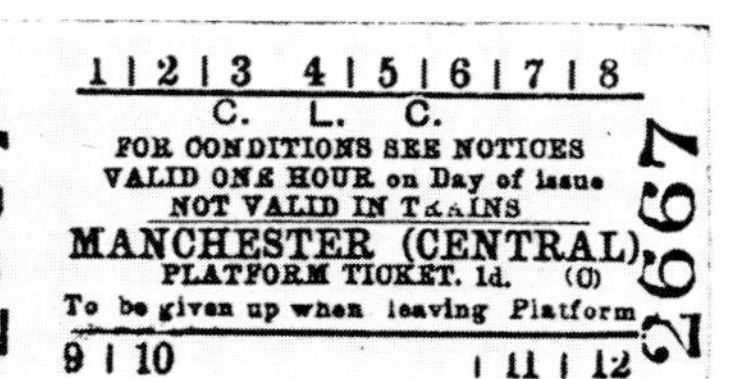

1 | 2 | 3 4 | 5 | 6 | 7 | 8
C. L. C.
2667 FOR CONDITIONS SEE NOTICES 2667
VALID ONE HOUR on Day of issue
NOT VALID IN TRAINS
MANCHESTER (CENTRAL)
PLATFORM TICKET. 1d. (O)
To be given up when leaving Platform
9 | 10 | 11 | 12

60. Central, 2nd May 1969. One of the last few departures from platform four may well have been this dmu bound for Warrington via Irlam, Flixton and Glazebrook. Re-routing of these services to Oxford Road took place upon closure, together with trains to Liverpool. Standing unattended for many years after closure, the vast iron and glass structure had suffered from a lack of maintenance. Timely but expensive conversion to the splendid and much needed exhibition centre known as "G-Mex" has seen the building survive with restoration on a grand scale, perhaps in a manner undreamed of by the original promoters.

Photo: M. S. Welch

61. Central, 12th May 1959. From a lofty perch high up in a corner of Central's arched roof the photographer gives a virtually unimpared view of the activities across the six platforms, numbered from right to left. Only a view such as this reveals the true architectural splendour of the magnificent roof span of 210 feet, with the highest point of the arch 90 feet above rail level. Between each platform face are three sets of lines, the central one of each being a "release road" to enable locomotives to depart freely without causing disruption after arriving with empty stock or departing after bringing in a train. To the left a 2-6-4 tank engine reverses away from platform six after delivering the empty stock of what is almost certainly a St. Pancras-bound express. On Platform five, a six coach train of corridor stock awaits the arrival of a locomotive as passengers steadily board the train. To the right of the second coach of this train is a tall glass display case which housed a fine model of the ship "Ben Machree", favourite of many holidaymakers on the Isle of Man Service. Beyond the wall to the right was the stations goods yard, a modest affair compared with that at London Road. However, it was on this site that the temporary station existed from 1877 until the opening on 1st July 1880 of the permanent one. Along the carriageway between platforms three and two can be seen many parcels trolleys that were used to carry a myriad of items — long before the days of "Red Star". In evidence also are mailbags, the once familiar wicker baskets, packing cases, tea chests and bundles of newspapers, all awaiting transport to far flung destinations, doubtless beyond the boundaries of the old CLC. *Photo: British Rail*

62. Central, 13th May 1965. A visitor to the new exhibition hall would find it hard to believe that trains ever penetrated that monumental hall. The ever familiar outline of a Stanier Class 5 No. 45139 is evident alongside platform five with the 1.45p.m. stopping train to Chinley via Stockport Tiviot Dale. This service provided a connection at Chinley with the 2.00p.m. Manchester Central to Nottingham train which had travelled via Cheadle Heath. It also went forward to Sheffield Midland via the Hope Valley. *Photo: P. E. Baughan*

C. L. C. For conditions see back | C. L. C. For conditions see back
THIRD CLASS SINGLE | THIRD CLASS SINGLE
5331 | 5331
Manchester(C.) | Manchester(C.)
Manchester(Cen) To
(C) DIDSBURY (C)
Didsbury | Didsbury
1/11 Z FARE 1/11 Z

63. Central, 12th March 1954. The highlights of Central's passenger services were surely the expresses to London St. Pancras. Made up in the nineteen fifties, to around eight coaches, these trains reflected the lightweight style of their Midland Railway forerunners. Jubilee Class 4-6-0 No. 45614 *Leeward Islands* has the benefit of a strong seasonal wind behind her as she pulls away with an express for the south.

The summer timetable for 1954 shows the fastest time to St. Pancras as being four hours and fourteen minutes, provided by the 7.20a.m. train ex Central. Although this was substantially slower than the best time on the former LNWR route from London Road, the beautiful and spectacular Peak District scenery was more than adequate compensation for most travellers. *Photo: B. K. B. Green*

64. (Centre) Central, 26th May 1954. A familiar sight beneath the arched roof in the nineteen-fifties were the former Great Central "Director" 4-4-0's of both D10 and D11 classes, trains to Chester via Northwich, and station pilot duty, being a penchant of these superb veterans. Pictured here is No. 62653 *Sir Edward Fraser*, one of the earlier D10's of 1913 and identifiable by the lack of side windows in the cab, moving a rake of empty coaching stock from a London train away from platform six and on to the carriage sidings at Cornbrook.

Photo: B. K. B. Green

65. (Below) Central, 12th May 1959. Contemporary with the interior *birds eye* view is this exterior of the station throat taken from the signal box. At this time Central had been re-signalled with theatre-type route indicators provided and new multiple aspect colour-lights. Platforms two and three, to the left foreground, have been extended and a substantial amount of fresh ballast is evident. To the right of the main train shed were platforms eight and nine which, along with bay platform seven, were an extension to the original station. In the bay (No. 7) an ex-LNER Class L1 2-6-4 tank engine with express headcode, is ready to take a three coach train over the Fallowfield line up to Guide Bridge where it will be attached to an electrically hauled train for Sheffield via Woodhead. It was originally intended, under phase four of the Manchester, Sheffield and Wath Electrification Scheme, to bring the catenary into Central via Fairfield and Chorlton Junctions, but unfortunately the project did not materialize, the wires only reaching the traction depot at Reddish. To the extreme right in platform nine, a Fowler 2-6-4 tank awaits departure with a stopping passenger train whilst another member of the class waits for the road between platforms one and two. The tracks to the goods yard, seen here to the left, still house a few wagons and vans. From here the track entered the CLC goods warehouses that stood alongside Watson Street and Windmill Street, facing the Free Trade Hall. Standing prominently is the Town Hall, the hands of its clock showing ten past one. It is difficult to imagine from this scene that the station had slipped into the final decade of its existence. *Photo: British Rail*

66. Manchester Central, c.1963. Without a doubt, the most prestigous and glamorous train to grace any of Manchester termini in modern times was the *Midland Pullman*. Launched into service on 4th July 1960 – Pullman would have been pleased – the 6-car diesel electric sets brought the Manchester-London time to within a 3 ¼ hour schedule. The trains carried a striking two tone livery of Nanking blue and white with the gold and red Pullman crest on the front of the power cars. Leaving Central at 8.50a.m. the train called at Cheadle Heath before running non-stop to St. Pancras where it arrived at 12.03p.m. Evening return was at 6.10 with arrival back in Manchester at 9.21, again with a stop at Cheadle Heath. The service was an instant success and brought British Railways a great deal of acclaim and publicity, crowds gathering along the lineside in south Manchester on those first summer evenings to watch the train speed by. *Photo: J. Clarke courtesy Greater Manchester Museum*

Below: Both sides of the publicity leaflet extolling the virtues of the Midland Pullman. The six-coach diesel-electric trains were something of a precursor to the highly successful High Speed Trains of today. Appropriately enough Pullman cars had made their debut on the Midland Railway nearly ninety years previously, setting standards of comfort for which their adoptive company became renowned. Sadly, the "Blue Pullmans" as they became known, were fairly short lived, being withdrawn from the Midland route in April 1966 following the introduction on the 10th of that month of the electrically hauled Pullman services between Euston and Piccadilly. In 1967 the sets were transferred from the LMR to work services out of Paddington to Bristol and South Wales along with the Western Region's existing eight coach sets. With the advent of Mk 2 stock the role of the Pullman trains was said to be limited and all five were withdrawn from service in 1973.

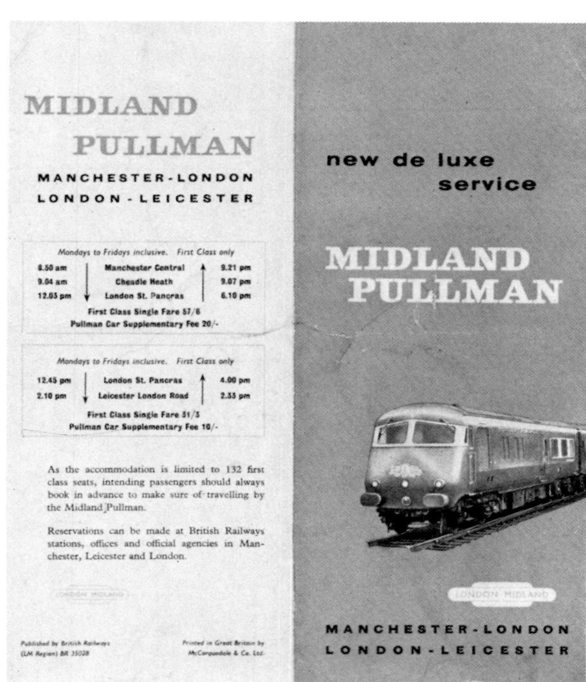

MIDLAND PULLMAN

MANCHESTER-LONDON
LONDON-LEICESTER

Mondays to Fridays inclusive. First Class only

8.50 am	Manchester Central	9.21 pm
9.04 am	Cheadle Heath	9.07 pm
12.03 pm	London St. Pancras	6.10 pm

First Class Single Fare 57/6
Pullman Car Supplementary Fee 20/-

Mondays to Fridays inclusive. First Class only

12.45 pm	London St. Pancras	4.00 pm
2.10 pm	Leicester London Road	2.35 pm

First Class Single Fare 51/3
Pullman Car Supplementary Fee 10/-

As the accommodation is limited to 132 first class seats, intending passengers should always book in advance to make sure of travelling by the Midland Pullman.

Reservations can be made at British Railways stations, offices and official agencies in Manchester, Leicester and London.

LONDON MIDLAND

Published by British Railways (LM Region) BR 35028

Printed in Great Britain by McCorquodale & Co. Ltd.

new de luxe service

MIDLAND PULLMAN

LONDON MIDLAND

MANCHESTER-LONDON
LONDON-LEICESTER

MIDLAND PULLMAN

MANCHESTER-LONDON
LONDON-LEICESTER

These trains are the latest word in luxury, comfort and speed which British Railways now offer. They have been specially designed with the inter-city travel requirements of the modern businessman principally in mind.

The coaches are most distinctive in appearance and the elegant decor of the interiors is restful and relaxing to the traveller. All passenger accommodation is fully air conditioned. There are roomy individual reclining seats, adjustable at the touch of a small lever.

The windows have double glazing, with venetian blinds between the two panes of glass. There is double insulation against sound and heat, in fact everything possible has been done for the traveller's comfort.

The menus are specially arranged each day and the wine list has been very carefully selected. The food is prepared in kitchens equipped with the most modern appliances.

The staff of the Midland Pullman will do everything they can to add to the pleasure of your journey and to maintain the traditionally high ideals of Pullman service.

Photographs
Top
The restful and luxurious parlour car.
Centre
A feature of the service is the first class cuisine.
Bottom
Meals and refreshments come to your table.

67. Manchester Central, 19th November 1963. Despite being a modern train and forerunner of later high speed rail travel, passengers travelling on the "Midland Pullman" were still ushered past this ancient and well-scuffed ticket barrier! Here a young lady, apparently returning from some kind of broadcasting assignment, has her first-class ticket dutifully checked. *Photo: British Rail*

68. (Above). Pullman service meant a meal at every seat. Here are the proud and capable gentlemen who provided them – resplendent in their uniforms on platform 6.
Photo: G. K. Fox Collection

9. (Below) Central, July 1960. Seen here longside platform six, this may well have een the Midland Pullman's press and lemonstration run on Friday 1st July judging by the immaculate "ex-works" finish.
Photo: Thompson Allied Newspapers

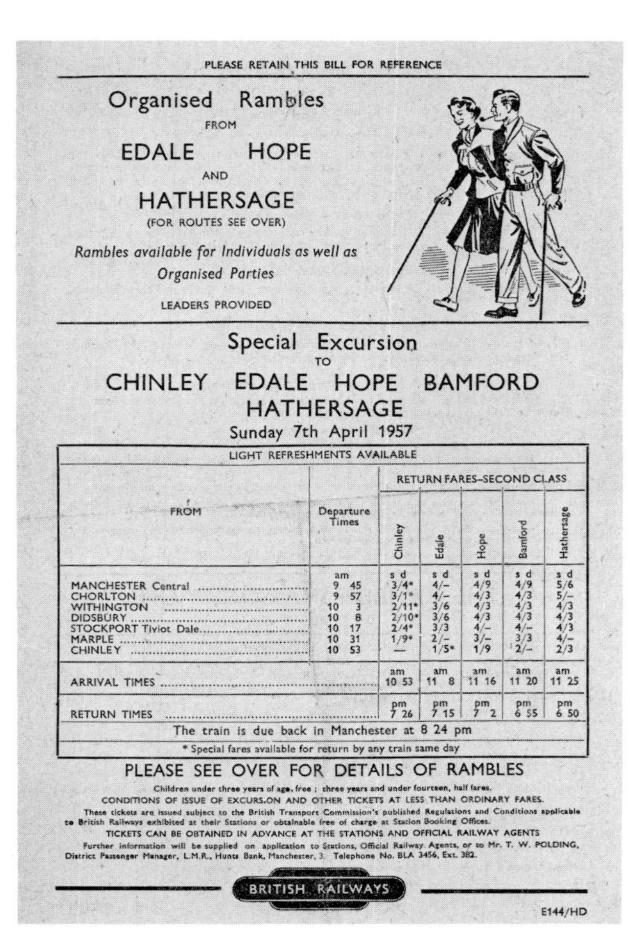

PLEASE RETAIN THIS BILL FOR REFERENCE

Organised Rambles
FROM
EDALE HOPE
AND
HATHERSAGE
(FOR ROUTES SEE OVER)

Rambles available for Individuals as well as Organised Parties

LEADERS PROVIDED

Special Excursion
TO
CHINLEY EDALE HOPE BAMFORD
HATHERSAGE
Sunday 7th April 1957

LIGHT REFRESHMENTS AVAILABLE

FROM	Departure Times	Return Fares–Second Class: Chinley	Edale	Hope	Bamford	Hathersage
	am	s d	s d	s d	s d	s d
MANCHESTER Central	9 45	3/4*	4/–	4/9	4/9	5/6
CHORLTON	9 57	3/1*	4/–	4/3	4/3	5/–
WITHINGTON	10 3	2/11*	3/6	4/3	4/3	4/3
DIDSBURY	10 8	2/10*	3/6	4/3	4/3	4/3
STOCKPORT Tiviot Dale	10 17	2/4*	3/3	4/–	4/–	4/3
MARPLE	10 31	1/9*	2/–	3/–	3/3	4/–
CHINLEY	10 53	—	1/5*	1/9	2/–	2/3
ARRIVAL TIMES		am 10 53	am 11 8	am 11 16	am 11 20	am 11 25
RETURN TIMES		pm 7 26	pm 7 15	pm 7 2	pm 6 55	pm 6 50

The train is due back in Manchester at 8 24 pm

* Special fares available for return by any train same day

PLEASE SEE OVER FOR DETAILS OF RAMBLES

Children under three years of age, free ; three years and under fourteen, half fares.

CONDITIONS OF ISSUE OF EXCURS.ON AND OTHER TICKETS AT LESS THAN ORDINARY FARES.

These tickets are issued subject to the British Transport Commission's published Regulations and Conditions applicable to British Railways exhibited at their Stations or obtainable free of charge at Station Booking Offices.

TICKETS CAN BE OBTAINED IN ADVANCE AT THE STATIONS AND OFFICIAL RAILWAY AGENTS

Further information will be supplied on application to Stations, Official Railway Agents, or to Mr. T. W. POLDING, District Passenger Manager, L.M.R., Hunts Bank, Manchester, 3. Telephone No. BLA 3456, Ext. 382.

BRITISH RAILWAYS

E144/HD

Above: Half size reproduction of a handbill advertising half day extensions from Central.

70. (Above) Manchester Central, c.1910. Lines of classic simplicity are displayed by Great Central Railway Class 11A (D6) 4-4-0 No. 866 seen in typically gleaming pre-Group condition alongside platform nine with a stopping passenger train. Number 866 was built by the celebrated Manchester firm of Beyer Peacock in 1899 to haul lightweight expresses on the GC's London Extension. The platform at which the train is standing formed part of an enlargement to the station which was completed in 1906 and had its own entrance from Lower Mosley Street. Notice that the canopy has straight fluted valancing and compare with the arched profile along the edge of platform eight. Somewhat ironically, these two platforms were the first to be taken out of use and were closed on 19th December 1967 along with the line between known as siding 'D'.

Photo: Railway Revivals

71. (Centre) Manchester Central, post-1927. The pioneer GC Class 9P (LNER B3) 4-6-0 No. 6169 *Lord Faringdon* backs out of the station with a train of empty coaching stock led by a Cheshire Lines Committee vehicle and carrying the varnished wood finish favoured by the joint concern. The photograph can be dated as post-1927, before which the six engines of the class were allocated to the Great Northern main line and worked from Kings Cross on Leeds expresses. In the background, one of Central's signal boxes is framed by a gantry of semaphore signals which disappeared as a result of re-signalling with colour-lights in June 1935. The three boxes controlling the station were replaced by a single concrete structure standing astride the approach lines and seen in the picture below.

Photo: J. M. Bentley Collection

72. (Right) Manchester Central, c.1958. In complete contrast to the earlier CLC signalbox with hipped and slated roof was the concrete and steel structure located over the lines to and from platforms 5, 6 and 7. This 1935 creation is seen to effect as Britannia Class No. 70015 *Apollo* arrives with the down "Palatine" in the summer of 1958. It was in the spring of that year that "Pacific" type motive power came to the St. Pancras-Manchester services in the shape of six of these fine locomotives, the biggest engines by far to ply the route on a regular basis. The "Palatine" was the only named train on the ex-Midland line to Manchester in post war years, the name originating on a 1938 morning express which left Central at 10a.m. In 1957 the title was resurrected and applied to a train in both directions. Northbound, the working left St. Pancras at 7.55a.m., stops being made at Luton, Wellingborough, Leicester, Derby, Matlock and Millers Dale before arrival in Manchester at 11.45. Pacific power not withstanding, the timing was still fifteen minutes longer than the pre-war "Peak Express", the fastest time available in those days over this splendid route.

Photo: W. Johnson

73. Manchester Victoria, c.1963/64. Approaching the station from Todd Street, the south east elevation of the massive Dawes facade greets the intending traveller, its stonework blackened by more than half a century of northern industrial grime. To the right of Lloyds Bank is Long Millgate from which there was a side entrance known as "cigar alley", a title which would seem to state the obvious but for which there has never been a full explanation. The buildings here were part of the 1905-9 enlargement and in railway circles is still known as the "new" station.

Photo: British Rail

74. (Below) Victoria, c.1955. After entering the station from the Long Millgate end platforms 1-10 are immediately encountered on the right, the area has changed little over the years save for the peripheral refurbishment and relocating of the numerous kiosks. In the distance can be seen the famous dome which originally presided over a restaurant built on the site of an earlier extension of the station in 1865. As the signs clearly indicate, the platforms along here served local trains for Heywood, Bury, Middleton, Oldham, Royton, Shaw, Ashton and Stalybridge, to name but a few.

Photo: V. R. Anderson Collection

75. (Below right) Victoria, 9th March 1958. Between platforms seven and eight was this novel and obviously well made piece of Lancashire and Yorkshire Railway furniture. These destination indicators were well known at the larger stations of the "Lanky" system. Notice the luggage bridge in the background spanning the platforms at right angles with hydraulic lift down to ground level.

Photo: T. Wray

76. Manchester Victoria, 29th May 1959. The intensive commuter services which used the terminal platforms which were very literally, a *dead* end. This part of the station has origins of a somewhat macabre nature, as the platforms were built over the Walkers Croft cemetery which the Manchester and Leeds Railway had purchased as far back as 1846. Alongside platform ten we see one of the five named Class 5 locomotives No. 45154 *Lanarkshire Yeomanry* impatiently "blowing-off" as she awaits departure with the 5.18p.m. stopping train to Rochdale, a fifty-minute journey which included stops at Miles Platting, Dean Lane, Failsworth, Hollinwood, Oldham Werneth, Oldham Central, Oldham Mumps, Royton Junction, Shaw and Crompton, New Hey and Milnrow. The rather austere cladding of the train shed had come about following damage inflicted during the Second World War and which resulted in the cutting back of the roof towards the platform ends. *Photo: R. Keeley*

77. (Centre) Victoria East Junction, July 1931. An avoiding line known as the "Manchester Loop" was opened on the 4th November 1877 from Victoria East Junction to Thorpes Bridge Junction, bypassing Miles Platting and therefore relieving pressure on the Hunts Bank incline. Until 1962 this section was signalled with semaphores and manually operated from the eighty-five lever L&Y built box at East Junction. This view shows the loop lines curving away to the left of the signal box towards Cheetham Hill Junction and Red Bank carriage sidings.

Coming off the loop line is a stopping train from Leeds hauled by Hughes 4-6-0 No. 10412 whilst the Lancashire and Yorkshire flavour is further enhanced by the unending variety of signalling equipment.

Some three decades later, the scene would change quite dramatically as a new East Junction signal box would appear to coincide with the introduction of modern equipment. On 2nd April 1962, the new signal box assumed control of lines formerly dealt with by Millgate (on the right of the picture), Turntable, Newtown No's 1 and 2 and footbridge boxes, as well as the old East Junction itself. *Photo: E. R. Morten*

78. (Below) Victoria East Junction, c.1956. This view on the east side of Victoria looks back towards the station from an elevated position on the incline. Relaying of the junction has resulted in the lines being possessed by the District Engineer. The unmistakeably square bodied stock of the Bury electric service is to be seen on the left of the picture. The incline between Victoria and Miles Platting was subject to several widening schemes as time progressed but the original lines into the station in 1844 approximately follow the alignment of the third and fourth tracks from the right. *Photo: C. Weir*

79 & 80. Victoria. Safety has always been of paramount importance on the railway. A control office was set up at Victoria in 1915 to monitor and organise, initially, the movement of freight trains within that area. The views to the left and right 79a and 79b shows the controllers at their positions in front of the system maps, sometime during the 1920's. The two centre photographs 80a and 80b show the Signalling School, also at Victoria, initiated by the L and Y in 1910 to teach methods of operation to potential signalmen. The view to the right shows Inspector Clifford Weir supervising one of the trainees.

81. Manchester Victoria, Hunts Bank. The rather foreboding and smoke-blackened exterior of the L&Y's former parcel office on the Hunts Bank approach to Victoria Station sometime before the First War. The company handled over 860,000 parcels a year at one time. A new office to handle this traffic opened on the far side of Victoria in 1894 when the buildings here reverted to use as offices. They remained as such until 1978 when demolition took place under the GMC's improvement scheme which revealed the celebrated Chetham's School, to the right of the picture, in all its splendour. The eye-catching poster hoarding advertises several contemporary delights. Blackpool is described as the 'City (sic) of Autumn Joys' – special Autumn attractions are billed as: 'dancing, theatres, merry carnivals and Sunday concerts'. The L&Y also seem keen to promote Southport and Morecambe as places worthy of visiting. Prospective travellers are reminded of the facilities at the former's Chapel Street station and are informed that the Grill Room has been recently enlarged and that the Cafe has 'moderate charges'.

Photo: National Railway Museum

82. Victoria, 1957. Here they come! With a good head of steam built up in readiness for the onslaught of Miles Platting bank, Class 2P 4-4-0 No. 40631 and rebuilt Patriot Class No. 45521 *Rhyl* head out of Exchange and eastwards through Victoria. The train is a Liverpool to Newcastle express which at the time made Exchange their port of call before continuing via Huddersfield, Leeds and York. In the summer of 1952 there were three trains each way on weekdays, the quickest time between Lime Street and Exchange being 47 minutes with a further 85 minutes allowed for the next stage to Leeds. In 1928/29, the LMS re-signalled the station precincts at Exchange and Victoria with multiple aspect colour light signalling. Concurrently, number eleven platform at Victoria and number three at Exchange were joined to form one continuous length which made it one of the longest railway platforms in the world. To the extreme left in the distance is the signal box at Victoria West Junction, one of three new boxes, including Deal Street and Irwell Bridge Sidings that replace six others. The new West Junction box contained 95 levers, electrically operated in place of the previous manual affair. *Photo: W. Johnson*

83. Victoria, c.1955. To provide banking assistance up the 1 in 47 grade to Miles Platting, two locomotives maintained a constant vigil on what was known locally as the *wall side* adjacent to the down slow road between platforms 11 and 12. For many years ex L and Y 0-6-0s could be seen fulfilling this role, occasionally interspersed with the odd 4F 0-6-0. In this scene the two old faithfuls are 52341 and 52431, a pleasing coincidence of numbers.

Both engines were built to a design by the then locomotive superintendent John Aspinall, the first in the class appearing in 1889. The design was perpetuated in further production of this class until 1917. Number 52431 was built in 1901 as L&YR 1148 and rebuilt in 1913 with Belpaire firebox and extended smokebox. Withdrawal took place in November 1959. The rear engine, No 52341, was built in 1896 as L&YR 350 and remained unaltered, save for superficial changes, until its withdrawal from stock in November 1960.

Until major alterations in the early nineteen thirties, Victoria had an overall roof, which covered all the tracks at this point. The large screen seen here was erected to keep the elements from passengers following the removal of the overall roof. Its massive presence dominated views in the past of the station.

Photo: W. Johnson

84. Victoria, 1st August 1953. The last large tank engine design to be built in Britain by British Railways was its Standard Class 4 2-6-4 type introduced in 1951. Of handsome appearance, they bore a strong resemblance to the successful Stanier and Fairburn engines of the LMS. The platforms on this side of the station were numbered 12 to 17 and formed part of a large extension to the earlier Victoria. Opened in May 1884, the new platforms, with the exception of the present number 16, had their own booking offices and waiting rooms and were connected by subway reached by an inclined approach behind platform number five – later eleven.

Photo: B. K. B. Green

85. Victoria, 1957. Railway stations, always places of romance and fascination, seem to take on another dimension at night. In the days of steam, extra thrills were provided as oil lamps loomed out of the blackness to the accompaniment of thumping exhausts, plumes of steam and the shimmering glow, thrown backwards out of firehole doors. What memories are evoked here by the dramatic silhouette of Stanier 2-6-4 tank No. 42649 seen here against the backdrop of platform thirteen with an east-bound stopping passenger train. *Photo: W. Johnson*

86. (Centre) Victoria, c.1955. Large though Victoria station was, photographic locations were somewhat limiting, platform eleven possibly giving the greatest scope. On this occasion we observe an eight-coupled engine of Great Central Railway origin at the head of an unfitted freight train – note that the locomotive has no vacuum pipe – possibly en route from Dewsnap, near Guide Bridge, to Brindle Heath Sidings, a point west of Manchester on the Bolton line. The 2-8-0 locomotive No. 63681 was one of over five hundred built to J. G. Robinson's very successful freight design of 1911 for wartime service overseas during the years 1917-19. To the left is the banking engine provided to assist trains up to Miles Platting. On this occasion No. 52161 stands awaiting its next turn of duty. This 0-6-0 tender engine, built in 1892 as No. 1148 of the Lancashire and Yorkshire Railway, was rebuilt in 1912 with Belpaire firebox and extended smokebox, a conversion which saw it through to eventual withdrawal in October 1960. *Photo: R. Keeley*

87. (Below-right) Victoria, 23rd August 1954. A view east from the end of platform thirteen shows the island platform arrangements that formed the major extension to the station in 1884. In platform fourteen, Class B1 No. 61016 *Inyala*, a York engine, prepares to move its train off to the carriage sidings at Ordsall Lane. The train has traversed the Calder Valley line via Normanton, Wakefield and Rochdale, a route opened in 1841 by the Manchester and Leeds Railway that first linked the two cities. A Bradshaw timetable of 1839 shows the railway under construction but incomplete. Trains from the Manchester end used the terminus at Oldham Road and ran as far as Littleborough with stops at Mills Hill, Blue Pits (Castleton) and Rochdale. An hourly service left Manchester on the hour, apart from noon, from eight in the morning until seven in the evening. The fare to Rochdale was three shillings (First Class), two shillings (Second Class) and one shilling (Third Class). In modern times, most Trans-Pennine express services use the more direct and slightly later LNWR line via Stalybridge and Huddersfield. Travellers from York also had the benefit of Newcastle to Liverpool through services, long established and provided with special sets of coaching stock in pre-Group days. *Photo: B. K. B. Green*

91. (Opposite-right) Manchester Exchange, May 1969. The demise is imminent of a once familiar landmark. The massive train shed of Exchange Station, opened in 1884, is seen from the south side of Victoria Street adjacent to the Cathedral. The cleaner brickwork beneath the station sign indicates the location of the erstwhile main entrance, destroyed following wartime bombing. The station could be entered from three separate directions, one being Salford via Chapel Street, a second along Cathedral Approach and the third perhaps less obvious method by the carriageway between platforms 4 and 5. Closure from 5th May 1969 was commemorated by a special train which left Exchange for a tour of the lines around Manchester before finishing at Central, also closed at the same time. *Photo: G. H. Platt*

88. (Left-upper). **Manchester Exchange. March 1964.** On the famous long platform 11 a Stanier Class 8 freight locomotive No.**48332** stands at the head of a parcels train whilst "Black Five" No.**45096** pulls into Exchange with a west bound passenger train. *D. Cousins.*

89. Exchange, 1940. Like many industrial cities, Manchester suffered badly in the Second World War at the hands of the enemy. Railways were obvious targets for aerial bombardment and on one night in 1940 the roof of Exchange Station scored a direct hit. Standing between platforms two and three, we look eastwards, the celebrated long platform to the left, towards Victoria to observe the chaos wrought by the attack. The gaping hole above platform one and the tons of debris scattered around provided the finer details of this rather poignant picture. It was as a result of this action that Exchange lost its rather fine Italianate fronted station building.
Photo: V. R. Anderson Collection

90. Exchange, 3rd August 1957. Cautiously taking the slow line towards Ordsall Lane carriage sidings is Jubilee Class locomotive No. 45708 *Resolution* of Farnley Junction (25G) shed with its train of empty coaching stock. The ends of the platforms are filled by the usual groups of "spotters", a familar sight throughout the country. *Photo: B. K. B. Green*

93. (Below) Exchange, 24th September 1965. Moving away from platform two is Stanier 4-6-0 Class 5 No. 45282 with the 4.30p.m. businessman's train to Llandudno. The popular North Wales resort had a history of prestige services going back to LNWR days the "Llandudno Club Train" being one of them. A pre-First World War innovation, this special train had the benefit of two 12-wheeled saloons which had been used on American boat trains between Euston and Liverpool. The "club" trains, serving such places as Blackpool, Southport, Windermere, and of course Llandudno, have progressively disappeared as the role of the businessman has changed.
Photo: W. J. Skillern

92. (Above) Exchange, August 1961. Dieselisation of Manchester's suburban services had begun in the mid-nineteen fifties, particularly on the north side. Here, alongside platform one is a Metropolitan Cammell 3-car set awaiting departure. *Photo: E. M. Johnson*

94. Exchange, February 1955. Although it was thought of as an appendage to Victoria, Exchange station possessed the usual peripherals in the way of public facilities. Having purchased a ticket the passenger was confronted by this Wymans kiosk opposite the ends of platforms one and two. Readers of more mature years will doubtless remember magazines such as *John Bull, Illustrated* and *Picture Post*, titles now long defunct. Of course, the well-read Mancunian always had the celebrated *Manchester Guardian*, seen advertised here, at his elbow. Above, the LNWR pattern signs, complete with pointing finger, leave passengers in no doubt as to the whereabouts of platforms 4 and 5. At the time this picture was taken one still encountered a sign directing travellers towards "Trains on the North Eastern Railway", a reminder of the through Liverpool to Newcastle services that called at Exchange up to closure.
Photo: British Rail

95. Liverpool Road, May 1956. There was little traffic to disturb the ghosts of Stephenson, Huskisson and Wellington when this picture of Manchester historic station was taken. The building occupied by Messrs Slaters, sausage manufacturers, was occupied by the Liverpool and Manchester Railway Company's agent for the station, Joseph Green, prior to the opening of the line, but is known to have existed beforehand. The second doorway was originally the first-class entrance to the station, the third and fourth doors providing access to second-class entrance and carriers office respectively. Beyond was a row of shops which unfortunately only saw limited use for their intended purpose. *Photo: G. H. Platt*

96. Liverpool Road, May 1956. Across Water Street at its junction with Liverpool Road was the city abbatoir and meat market. Part of this complex contained a pig market, the roof of which can be seen to the left. The markets were moved to new premises near Phillips Park in 1962, directly alongside the railway once again. The first bridge over Water Street carries the Liverpool and Manchester line of 1830 but reconstruction in 1904 saw removal of the ornate piers and parapets. Beyond is the bridge carrying the lines that served the warehouses – Grape Street and Lower Byrom Street. Since closure of Liverpool Road to goods traffic in 1975, the site has been extensively redeveloped to incorporate the Greater Manchester Museum of Science and Industry and an extension of facilities to Granada Television. Of particular interest to Mancunians are the bill boards to the left of the picture giving details of two of the towns favourite entertainment venues of the period. The Manchester Hippodrome at Ardwick has long since gone but the "Aces" are still to be seen at Belle Vue, albeit without the added attractions provided by the late and lamented amusement park. *Photo: G. H. Platt*

97. Liverpool Road, 12th May 1956. Liverpool Road, acknowledged as the 'oldest passenger railway' station in the world saw its services directed to Victoria as long ago as the 4th May 1844, concurrent with the latter's opening. Despite this loss though, the station flourished as a goods depot, general merchandise, dock and continental traffic being handled there. In this view towards Ordsall Lane, passenger traffic has returned, albeit only fleetingly, in the form of a Stephenson Locomotive Society/Manchester Locomotive Society enthusiasts railtour. Former LYR 0-6-0 No. 52438 stands outside the 1830 terminal building having traversed the 25 chains from Ordsall Lane. *Photo: B. Hilton*

98. Salford, 26th September 1976. Tucked away to the western side of New Bailey Street between two bridge abutments was the rather uninspiring entrance to Salford station, originally opened in 1839 as the Manchester terminus of the Bolton and Manchester line following an act of parliament dated 23rd August 1831 giving the Manchester, Bolton and Bury Canal and Railway Company powers to drain the canal and construct a railway. Subsequent amendments resulted in much of the canal remaining, certainly as far as the Oldfield Road, area. The original terminal building on the east side of New Bailey Street shared the site of the present centre bridge and disappeared when the line was extended over the road and into Victoria in 1865. The station entrance shown here resulted from the widening of the line, again to Victoria in 1895. The third bridge at the station, on the south side, carries the former LNWR line from Ordsall Lane, opened in 1844, to link up with the Manchester and Leeds at Hunts Bank. This bridge however was reconstructed in the late 1880's

Photo: T. Wray

99. (Below) Salford, c.1959. This view west from a Manchester bound train shows the island platforms, numbered 3 and 4. The station was enlarged in the 1890's to the form we see here with the standardized Lancashire and Yorkshire Railway buildings beneath large glazed canopies. Access to the five platforms was by inclined ramps down to the entrance in New Bailey Street. Until the enlargement, the station possessed three platforms, one of which (No. 1) was a bay traditionally serving trains for the East Lancashire lines.

Photo: G. H. Platt

100. (Bottom) Ordsall Lane, c.1959. Empty and dilapidated buildings are all that remain of Ordsall Lane station in this poignant view from the south side. Though not qualifying under the broad heading as a city centre station, Ordsall Lane was one of Manchester's first suburban stations albeit situated in Salford! It was from this location on 4th May 1844 that the Liverpool and Manchester Railway opened their line into Victoria to link up with the Manchester and Leeds organization. The station, situated between Oldfield Road and Wilburn Street bridges had five through platforms which were connected by a subway from the entrance on Middlewood Street.

The line from London Road to Ordsall Lane opened on 1st August 1849 to link the Liverpool and Manchester line with the Manchester and Birmingham line. It is unclear if Ordsall Lane station opened at this time although the name appeared in *Bradshaw* for October 1849. In connection with the building of Exchange Station and increase in capacity of lines immediately west of Manchester between 1882 and 1884 Ordsall Lane was enlarged although essentially it was only served by local trains operating between Exchange and other South Lancashire towns. Under the LNWR most of its business was provided by the service to Bolton (Great Moor Street) which continued on a spasmodic basis until closure of that route to passengers in 1954. Saturdays provided an escape route for the local population with trains to Windermere. Closure came on 4th February 1957, presumably as an economy measure but possibly surprising in view of the eight east-bound trains which called before 9.30 in the morning. Ordsall Lane was also the site of an engine shed which the Liverpool and Manchester had established back in 1830. However, this was superceded by larger premises in 1864, a facility which lasted until 1904 when nearby Patricroft was enlarged.

Photo: G. H. Platt

101. Manchester London Road, 15th January 1959. This man made scene of devastation is just three and a half months following closure of the line between London Road and Oxford Road stations to enable modernization of the railway. The large wrought iron girders to the left carried the tracks over Fairfield Street whilst the three workmen stand in a void that was formerly the island platform for the South Junction lines. Its place was to be taken by the pre-stressed concrete structure described in plate 47. The line between here and Oxford Road reopened to traffic from Monday 25th April 1960.

Photo: H. Bedford

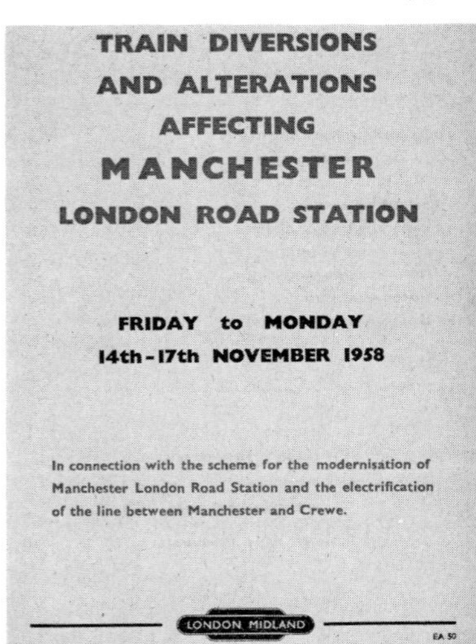

TRAIN DIVERSIONS
AND ALTERATIONS
AFFECTING
MANCHESTER
LONDON ROAD STATION

FRIDAY to MONDAY
14th-17th NOVEMBER 1958

In connection with the scheme for the modernisation of Manchester London Road Station and the electrification of the line between Manchester and Crewe.

LONDON MIDLAND

EA 50

102. Manchester London Road, 1959. The left wing of the 1866 building still remains to reveal the end screens of the train shed's south side in all their smoke-blackened glory. Passengers using London Road at the time may remember the temporary wooden booking and enquiry offices on the left of the station approach. The rounded features of the contemporary cars are a reminder of motoring in the days before the all pervading yellow lines.

Photo: British Rail

103. Manchester London Road, 1962. Confident signs of the new station now appear with the name *Piccadilly* visible on the contractors signboard. Christened "Tower Block", the new building was a mixture of glass, steel and concrete with foundations reaching a further forty or so feet below. Buildings such as these radically altered the face of Manchester in the nineteen sixties and the skyscraper appearance of the modern structure offers stark contrast to the remains of the nineteenth century station building below. It is appropriate to mention the trials and tribulations of railway staff throughout what was a monumental period of change. Spare a though for the driver and his mate, seen here on the right. Undoubtedly men of the steam era, they had to adapt to first diesel and then electric traction in a comparatively short space of time.

Photo: R. G. Chapman Collection

.04. Manchester London Road, 9th \pril 1960. With the demolition of the /ictorian offices and booking hall omplete, we have an uninterrupted iew north-westwards across Manhester. Clearly visible are the Assize Courts in Minshull Street, their fine Gothic proportions reminding us of he time when the city had many more plendid buildings than it does today. \lthough wisps of steam can be seen n the far corner of the picture, the mmediate subject is motive power of more modern kind. A Birmingham RC&W 3-car dmu waits to leave with he 3.50p.m. to Macclesfield (Hibel Road) via Stockport; one of two outes from Manchester to 'Silk Town' in those days. The LNWR's Hibel Road Station, inconveniently ituated for Macclesfield town, closed n November 1960. Services were then oncentrated on a newly rebuilt and nuch more convenient Macclesfield Central which had been hitherto used y the E.R. service referred to in Plate 4. Regrettably, this service ceased n January 1970 and trains from Picadilly on this line now terminate at Rose Hill (Marple). The section of tation to the right of the twin row of oof support columns forms the 1866 ortion whilst that to the left is part of he enlargement completed in 1882.

Photo: M. Mensing.

105. (Below) London Road, 23rd April 1960. An elevated view from the partially completed stairway to the new footbridge shows reconstruction work reaching an advanced state. At roof level re-glazing and re-painting are well under way as are the platform works which have created four new faces compared with the original three. This was formerly the LNER side of the station, electrified at 1500V DC since 1954 as part of the Manchester Sheffield and Wath scheme. Prospects of any trains arriving look decidedly doubtful but in fact the section of line between here and Ardwick was brought back into use two days later. The remaining platforms 5 to 10 which had been affected chiefly by track remodelling outside the station returned to full use from Monday 29th August 1960. *Photo: H. Bedford*

106. London Road, 9th April 1960. A view across the approaches of the station showing it in the final stages of transition. Overhead line trains complete the wiring ready for the first of the 25 kV AC electric trains. Electrification south to Crewe was inaugurated in the September of that year. In the foreground, features such as semaphore signals and water tanks will soon be things of the past but the focal point for the young train spotters is the English Electric 1-Co-Co-1 diesel electric locomotive D236 backing into platform 4 prior to taking the "Lancastrian" up to Euston. This named train had origins dating back to LMS days in 1927 and shared the same eminence of other Manchester Refreshment Car Expresses such as the *Comet* and *Mancunian.* Notice the contemporary school "fashions" of blazers, caps and long knitted socks, not an Anorak or pair of "trainers" to be seen!

Photo: M. Mensing

107. Piccadilly, 27th September 1960. The clock on platform 4 says 2.28, the roof columns may be 19th century but, beneath, all is brand new. Alongside freshly built platforms stands the very latest in BR motive power. In front are Bo-Bos AL1 E3002 and AL2 E3048 which have arrived with the 8.55 express ex Cardiff; down by the buffers, another AL1 No. E3004 completes the trio. For those of us who remember the inauguration of these fine machines it is good to know that (as Class 81) they are expected to give several years of useful service yet.

Photo: M. Mensing

108. Piccadilly, 27th September 1960. Type AL3 (Class 83) No. E3024 (83.001) was the first of this type to emerge from Vulcan Foundry and was just over two months old when this picture was taken. The train, the 6.00p.m. to Birmingham, is waiting to leave platform 6. It is interesting to reflect that the driver, Fred Burley, from Longsight Depot, would probably have started his railway career around the time of the First World War. Weaned on steam, re-trained to handle Diesels and then electric, the upheaval and tribulations faced by footplate crews in those days of change is often, sadly, overlooked. *Photo: M. Mensing*

109. Manchester Oxford Road, 1961. The first flush of modernization was completed in 1960 but it was another ten years before alterations to the MSJ&A route enabled through running of trains betweeen Altrincham and Crewe via Piccadilly. Seen here early in this interim period is a green liveried 25 kV AC Class 304 electric multiple unit awaiting departure for Alderley Edge. In the bay platform (4) to the left, one of the 1931 LMS built 1500V DC trains, specially produced for the MSJ&A, awaits the right away for Altrincham. Under the rebuilding programme Oxford Road was provided with five platforms. two serving Altrincham trains (5 and 4), one for Crewe line services and the remaining pair (2 and 1) for through workings. Further upheaval was to affect the station in the next decade, chiefly through the closure of Manchester Central. The scheme involved extensive permanent way and civil engineering works which once again changed the face of Oxford Road. A new platform (No. 1) was provided on the down or south side – above New Wakefield Street. Platforms 1, 2, 3 and 4 were renumbered 2, 3, 4 and 5 respectively and the former platform 5 removed. The revised arrangement was far reaching, giving bi-directional working on platforms 1 to 4 and on the up and down lines between Piccadilly and Oxford Road. A new facing crossover at Knott Mill enabled trains routed into 2, 3 and 4 platforms via the down as well as the up lines. Work had also been proceeding on a new signalling scheme to extend the control of London Road power signal box. As well as allowing for the closure of Central the area was being extended to Trafford Park Junction on the former CLC line to Liverpool and Warwick Road station on the Altrincham line. Upon closure of Central from 5th May 1969, the scheme was commissioned. Conversion of the MSJ&A from 1500V DC overhead to the 25 kV 50 HZ AC system was finalised at 06.00 on Monday 3rd May 1971 after re-energisation at the higher voltage.

Photo: British Rail

110. (Below) Manchester Oxford Road, 13th March 1959. Some six months after commencement of work, the new station begins to take shape as we see Oxford Road in the throes of rebuilding for the second time this century. This almost aerial like view of the reconstruction, seen from a point high up in the adjacent Refuge Assurance building, shows the "Altrincham" bay platforms 4 and 5 at an advanced stage. These platforms would remain in use by the MSJ&A trains, energised at 1500V DC, whilst the rest of the station and the line to London Road (Piccadilly), following extensive engineering works, would acquire equipment for 25 kV AC operation. The old station, in the lower left of the picture is still substantially intact. To the right, Whitworth Street West runs alongside the new bay platforms and mention of the "Ritz" ballroom will evoke memories to many. Out of sight at this point but very much in evidence, is the Rochdale Canal, described in nineteenth century literature as *black and filthy*. In recent times however, the canal has been cleaned up and pleasure craft provide a regular sight. Just by the bend in Whitworth Street West is the widened bridge over the junction with Cambridge Street. A then familiar sight to the left of the line are the gasholders at the Gaythorn gas works, which were once rail connected and now all but obliterated. Returning to the station the skeletal form of the conoid or "armadillo" shaped structure of the new station rises, mushroom-like in the centre.

The buildings of the old station, including those on the island platform, had all been demolished by the Spring of 1960.

Photo: British Rail

111. Manchester Oxford Road, 21st June 1961. Looking west from a point above Oxford Road itself we see the rebuilt station still with the new look about it. The famous but controversial "Armadillo" roof is prominent, the timber frontage providing a pleasing contrast to the unbroken expanses of concrete.

In 1986 it became possible to travel to Hull from Oxford Road via the new chord line at Hazel Grove and the Dore and Chinley or "Hope Valley" line to Sheffield. Something of a "quart into a pint pot", Oxford Road has developed from a station of relatively minor importance to a focal point in Manchester's railway system. Future traffic levels are set to increase with the projected "Windsor Link" which will allow trains from places such as Bolton, Preston and Scotland to serve Piccadilly directly and provide many useful connections and new journeys. *Photo: British Rail*

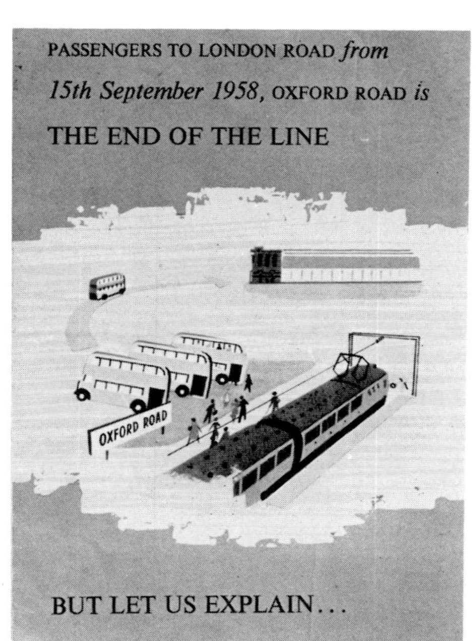
PASSENGERS TO LONDON ROAD *from 15th September 1958*, OXFORD ROAD *is* THE END OF THE LINE

BUT LET US EXPLAIN...

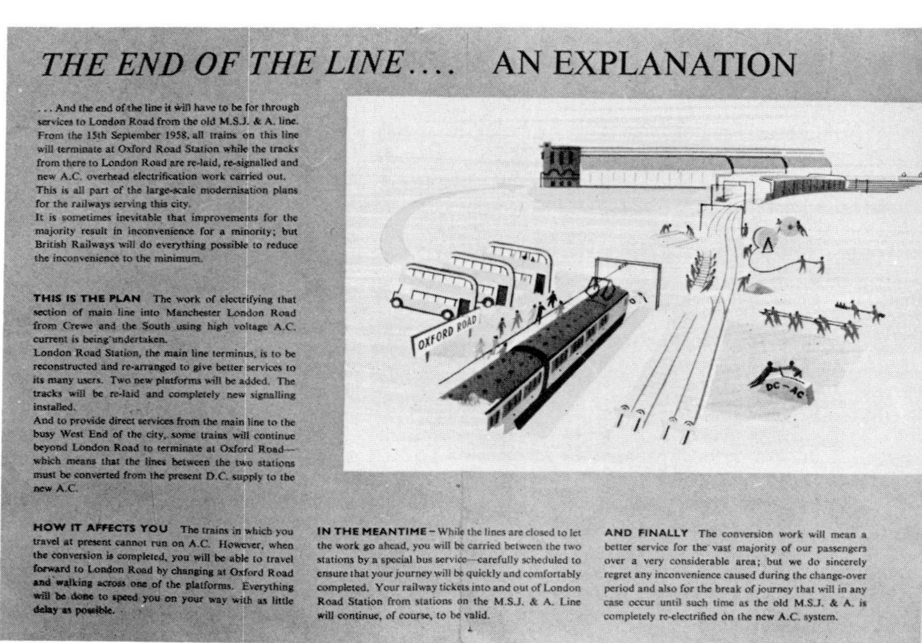
THE END OF THE LINE.... AN EXPLANATION

. . . And the end of the line it will have to be for through services to London Road from the old M.S.J. & A. line. From the 15th September 1958, all trains on this line will terminate at Oxford Road Station while the tracks from there to London Road are re-laid, re-signalled and new A.C. overhead electrification work carried out.
This is all part of the large-scale modernisation plans for the railways serving this city.
It is sometimes inevitable that improvements for the majority result in inconvenience for a minority; but British Railways will do everything possible to reduce the inconvenience to the minimum.

THIS IS THE PLAN The work of electrifying that section of main line into Manchester London Road from Crewe and the South using high voltage A.C. current is being undertaken.
London Road Station, the main line terminus, is to be reconstructed and re-arranged to give better services to its many users. Two new platforms will be added. The tracks will be re-laid and completely new signalling installed.
And to provide direct services from the main line to the busy West End of the city, some trains will continue beyond London Road to terminate at Oxford Road—which means that the lines between the two stations must be converted from the present D.C. supply to the new A.C.

HOW IT AFFECTS YOU The trains in which you travel at present cannot run on A.C. However, when the conversion is completed, you will be able to travel forward to London Road by changing at Oxford Road and walking across one of the platforms. Everything will be done to speed you on your way with as little delay as possible.

IN THE MEANTIME – While the lines are closed to let the work go ahead, you will be carried between the two stations by a special bus service—carefully scheduled to ensure that your journey will be quickly and comfortably completed. Your railway tickets into and out of London Road Station from stations on the M.S.J. & A. Line will continue, of course, to be valid.

AND FINALLY The conversion work will mean a better service for the vast majority of our passengers over a very considerable area; but we do sincerely regret any inconvenience caused during the change-over period and also for the break of journey that will in any case occur until such time as the old M.S.J. & A. is completely re-electrified on the new A.C. system.

M. S. J. & A. R. BULK TRAVEL
0155
NOT TRANSFERABLE. This ticket is issued subject to the General Notices, Regulations & Conditions in the L.&N.E. & L.M.&S.Ry.Cos' current Time Tables, Book of Regulations and Bills.
Available for 3 days, including day of issue.
MANCHESTER (Oxford Rd.) to ALTRINCHAM and BOWDON (M.S.J.&A.)
THIRD CLASS
0155

112. Manchester Oxford Road. Throughout their life of almost four decades the MSJ&A electric trains were very popular almost to the point of being taken for granted. Looking back, they were a classic design that revolutionized travel on a much loved suburban railway. Although minimal in terms of journey time, today's Class 304 mu's take twenty two minutes to complete the eight mile trip compared with nineteen minutes in the nineteen-thirties. Contrasting with the view in plate 109, one of the "Altrincham" sets runs into platform four to complete its journey. *Photo: British Rail*

The next four pages include views between London Road and Levenshulme and are intended to provide a link with the first book in the series *The Railways around Stockport*. The appendices on each page give details of passenger train timetables for each of the terminal stations. Train departure times have been given preference.

113. Ardwick, September 1954. Ardwick, three quarters of a mile out from London Road, is the point where the former Great Central main line to Sheffield and Marylebone left that of the LNWR south to Stockport and Crewe. A second junction at Ardwick, immediately north of the station, enabled connections with the L&Y at Philips Park on the Ashton Branch to be made. The two mile "Ardwick Branch", as it was called was promoted by the Lancashire and Yorkshire Railway and also gave a connection to the Midland Railway at a junction appropriately named *Midland Junction*. This view towards Manchester is taken from the island platform and illustrates the staggered nature of the station layout dating from the 1860's. The island platform situation arose following further enlargement in the early years of this century when the loop line to the left was added. The inclined approach at the Ashburys end of the station was replaced by a wooden ramp built on to the newly constructed retaining wall. This facility served milk trains and the short tunnel beneath the railway at this point is still known as the "milk arch". Just to the right of the footbridge is a building latterly used for the servicing of carriages although early maps show it as an "engine" shed. School lunchtime visits to the station witnessed a small army of lady cleaners leaving their work around one o'clock. Interesting touches are provided by the GC's lattice post signals, unique to the section of the line between here and Hyde Junction which had been quadrupled by 1909. On the LNWR side of the tracks, a ticket platform had existed for checking down trains until about 1919. *Photo: B. K. B. Green*

Appendix 1 — **MANCHESTER LONDON ROAD (LNER SIDE) WEEKDAY DEPARTURES (From Working T/Table June 1947)**
(Does not include trains described as "suspended" or trains originating at London Road South Junction i.e.: coming off MSJ&A line).
A.M. 1.35 *Cleethorpes;* **4.25** *Marple via Reddish;* **5.10** *Glossop;* **5.45** *Hadfield;* **5.50** *Hayfield via Hyde;* **6.08** *Stalybridge;* **6.14** *Marple via Reddish;* **6.22** *Macclesfield (Central) via Hyde;* **6.30** *Hadfield;* **6.36** *Hayfield via Reddish;* **6.58** *Stalybridge;* **7.18** *Hayfield via Hyde;* **7.35** *Macclesfield (Central) via Reddish;* **7.52** *Marple via Reddish;* **8.25** *Marylebone;* **8.30** *Glossop;* **8.43** *Macclesfield (Central) via Hyde;* **9.00** *Lincoln;* **9.18** *Hayfield via Hyde;* **9.55** *Marylebone;* **10.00 SX** *Glossop;* **10.05 SO** *Glossop;* **10.35** *Macclesfield (Central) via Hyde,* **10.55** *Hadfield;* **10.49 SO** *Hayfield via Reddish;* **11.35 SO** *Marple via Reddish*

P.M. 12.05 SO *Cleethorpes;* **12.10 SO** *Hadfield;* **12.15** *Hayfield via Hyde;* **12.22 SO** *New Mills (Central) via Reddish;* **12.30** *Leicester;* **12.40 SO** *Hadfield;* **12.42 SO** *Macclesfield (Central) via Reddish;* **12.52 SO** *Macclesfield (Central) via Hyde;* **12.55 SX** *Macclesfield (Central) via Hyde;* **1.05 WO** *Marple via Reddish;* **1.05 SO** *Hayfield via Reddish;* **1.10 SX** *Glossop;* **1.25 SO** *Hadfield;* **1.30 SO** *Marple via Reddish;* **1.55 SO** *Macclesfield (Central) via Hyde;* **2.23** *Hayfield via Hyde;* **2.30 SO** *Marple via Reddish;* **2.38 SO** *Hadfield;* **2.43 SX** *Hadfield;* **3.05** *Macclesfield (Central) via Hyde;* **3.50** *Marylebone;* **3.52 SX** *Rose Hill via Reddish;* **4.10** *Hayfield via Hyde;* **4.25 SX** *Macclesfield (Central) via Reddish;* **4.42** *Hadfield;* **4.50 SX** *Marple via Reddish;* **5.00** *Cleethorpes;* **5.03** *Hayfield via Reddish;* **5.06 SX** *Marple via Hyde SO Hayfield via Hyde;* **5.11 SX** *Macclesfield (Central) via Reddish;* **5.17 SX** *Glossop;* **5.20** *Hadfield;* **5.23** *Hayfield via Reddish;* **5.27 SX** *Hayfield via Hyde;* **5.35 SX** *Marple via Reddish;* **5.40 SX** *Stalybridge;* **5.45** *Macclesfield via Reddish.*

P.M. 5.50 SX *Rose Hill via Hyde;* **5.55 SX** *Hadfield;* **6.00** *Hayfield via Reddish;* **6.22** *Marple via Hyde;* **6.27 SX** *Rose Hill via Reddish;* **6.50** *Hayfield via Reddish;* **6.35 SX** *Hadfield;* **7.15** *Macclesfield (Central) via Reddish;* **7.40** *Marple via Hyde;* **7.45** *Hadfield;* **8.15** *Hayfield via Reddish;* **8.45** *Macclesfield (Central) via Hyde;* **9.25** *Hadfield;* **9.35** *Hayfield via Hyde;* **10.10 SO** *Glossop;* **10.20** *New Mills (Central) via Reddish;* **10.25** *Sheffield;* **10.45 SO** *Macclesfield via Reddish;* **10.58** *Hayfield via Hyde.*

Appendix 2 — **EXCHANGE: Working Time Table 21st September 1953 u.f.n.**
DEPARTURES — A.M. 1.10 *Wigan-Mails;* **10.45 SuO** *ex Leeds; 12.15 MX ex Stalybridge;* **2.5** *Wigan-Newspapers;* **2.55** *Bangor-Parcels;* **3.23** *St. Helens-Newspapers;* **5.50** *Preston via Wigan;* **6.5** *Earlstown;* **6.33 SX** *Bolton G;* **7.0** *Wigan NW;* **7.10** *Liverpool Lime Street;* **7.32** *Bolton GMS;* **7.50** *Chester;* **7.55** *Kenyon Junction;* **8.10** *Bolton GMS;* **8.25** *Liverpool LS, ex Leeds City;* **8.35** *Chester;* **9.0** *Liverpool LS, ex Leeds City;* **10.10** *Liverpool LS, ex Leeds City;* **10.25** *Chester;* **10.58** *Wigan NW;* **11.42** *Liverpool LS, ex Hull;* **11.55** *Llandudno.*

P.M. 12.5 SO *Kenyon Junction;* **12.15 SO** *Bolton GMS;* **12.20 SO** *St. Helens Jn;* **12.45 SO** *Wigan NW;* **12.53** *Liverpool LS, ex Newcastle;* **1.10 SO** *Earlstown;* **1.35** *Llandudno;* **1.40 TWO** *Patricroft-Parcels;* **1.40 SO** *Wigan NW;* **2.20** *Liverpool LS, ex Newcastle;* **3.15** *Wigan NW;* **3.20 SX** *St.Helens;* **3.48 SO** *St. Helens;* **3.55** *Barrow;* **4.5 SX** *Liverpool LS;* **4.15** *Preston NU;* **4.18** *Wigan NW;* **4.30 SX** *Llandudno;* **4.30 SO** *Chester;* **5.0** *Liverpool LS, ex Hull;* **5.5** *St. Helens;* **5.7 SX** *Chester;* **5.10 SX** *Windermere;* **5.15** *Liverpool LS;* **5.25 SX** *Bolton GMS;* **5.35** *Llandudno;* **5.40 SX** *Leigh;* **5.45** *Liverpool LS;* **6.6** *Wigan NW;* **7.22** *Chester;* **8.14** *St. Helens;* **8.49** *Liverpool LS, ex Newcastle;* **8.50 SO** *Bolton GMS;* **9.10** *Chester;* **9.20 SX** *Wigan NW;* **9.25 SO** *Wigan NW;* **9.50 SX** *Heysham-Newspapers;* **10.5 SO** *Wigan-Newspapers;* **10.15** *Leigh;* **10.20** *Holyhead;* **10.40** *Liverpool LS, ex Leeds City;* **10.45** *Wigan NW;* **11.10 SO** *Glasgow-Newspapers;* **11.20 SX** *Glasgow-Parcels.*

114. Longsight, 1958. Longsight station was adjacent to the site of Manchester's famous pleasure gardens so accordingly, the suffix "for Belle Vue' was attached to the station's title. Pulling away from the station is a stopping train to Stafford formed of a Metropolitan Cammell dmu in the familia all-over green livery of the period. The front end of the unit displays yellow "speed whiskers" and a prominent "B4" headcode indicates the fact that i is a Stafford working, a feature later abandoned. To the right, on the loop south of Longsight depot, a Fowler 2-6-4 tank emits a lazy plume of smok as it waits with a train of empty coaching stock. Alongside, is another diesel multiple unit, on this occasion of the Birmingham RC & W variety exhibiting a white roof end, hallmark of Buxton depot and still in evidence today. This wintry scene in 1958 shows the station surrounded b numerous terraced houses, many doubtlessly inhabited by railwaymen. The station itself closed on 15th September 1958, a victim of the extensive re modelling carried out between Slade Lane and London Road in connection with the electrification programme which began that year. Much ha changed in the area during the near 30 years since this photograph was taken. The terraced rows have given way to more modern housing and at th time of publication extensive development is taking place on the Belle Vue site. With the Freightliner depot now closed, could there once again, on wonders, be a station at Longsight?
Photo: M. S. Welc

Appendix 3 — **MAYFIELD June 5th — September 24th 1950**

DEPARTURES — A.M. **7.37 SO** *to Wilmslow via Styal;* **8.18 SO** *LE to Longsight – ex Heaton Norris;* **8.25 SX** *ECS to Stockport – ex Wilmslow train;* **8.50 ECS** *t Longsight – ex Wilmslow SO; Heaton Norris SX;* **9.20 ECS** *to Longsight – ex Heaton Norris SO; Wilmslow SX;* **9.53 DX** *LE to Longsight after shunting;* **9.55 ECS** *t Longsight – ex Chelford SX, Wilmslow SO;* **10.53** *SO Empty Vans to Longsight.*

P.M. **12.8 SO** *to Stockport – ex Heaton Norris, Wilmslow sets;* **12.24 SO** *to Wilmslow via Styal – ex Longsight CS;* **12.30 SO** *to Whaley Bridge – ex Longsight CS;* **1.** **SO** *to Stockport – ex Wilmslow;* **1.55 SX** *to Stockport; SO to Alderley Edge – ex Heaton Norris SX, Chelford SO;* **2.2 SO** *LE to Longsight – ex Wilmslow;* **2.10 SO** *LE t Longsight – ex Buxton;* **2.25** *to Buxton – ex Wilmslow;* **2.35 SO** *ECS to Stockport – ex Whaley Bridge;* **3.20** *to Crewe – ex Birmingham SX; Wilmslow SO;* **3.25 SO** *Empt Vans to Longsight – ex Stoke;* **3.35 SO** *Empty Vans to Longsight;* **4.2 SO** *to Buxton – ex Buxton;* **4.7 SO** *to Wilmslow via Styal – ex Stoke;* **4.15 SX** *to Wilmslow via Styal ex Wilmslow;* **4.17 SO** *ECS to Longsight – ex Swansea Victoria;* **4.20 SO** *to Uttoxeter – ex Stafford;* **4.28 SO** *to Crewe – ex Sandbach;* **4.48 SX** *ECS to Longsight CS – e Bournemouth;* **5.0 SX** *to Wilmslow via Styal – ex Wilmslow;* **5.5 SO** *to Buxton – ex Wilmslow;* **5.8 SX** *to Stockport – ex Heaton Norris;* **5.22 SO** *to Stoke – ex Longsigh CS;* **5.25 SX** *to Stockport – ex Wilmslow;* **5.33 FO** *ECS to Longsight CS – ex Paignton;* **5.53 SO** *to Wilmslow via Styal – ex Longsight CS;* **6.5 SO** *to Uttoxeter – e Longsight CS;* **6.5 SX** *to Stockport – ex Buxton;* **6.30** *to Crewe – ex Crewe SX; Longsight CS SO;* **6.34 SX** *LE to Longsight – ex Crewe;* **6.45** *to Wilmslow via Styal – e Stockport SO; Wilmslow SX;* **7.35** *to Wilmslow via Styal ex Macclesfield;* **8.20** *to Wilmslow via Styal – ex Wilmslow;* **9.6 SO** *to Buxton – ex Buxton SO; Wilmslow SX* **9.18 SO** *LE to Longsight – ex Crewe;* **10.45 FO** *LE to Longsight – ex Wilmslow;* **11.10 FO** *ECS to Longsight CS – ex Crewe.*

Appendix 4 — **MANCHESTER CENTRAL. Working Time Table — September 1953**

DEPARTURES — A.M. **12.05** *Derby MO. St. Pancras MX;* **4.30** *ECS;* **5.18 SX** *Warrington;* **5.18 SO** *Warrington;* **5.30 SX** *Risley;* **5.40** *ECS;* **5.55** *Chester;* **6.0** *Liverpool;* **6.05** *Buxton;* **6.20** *Warrington;* **6.50** *Liverpool;* **6.55 SX** *Cheadle Heath;* **7.10** *Liverpool;* **7.15** *St. Pancras;* **7.17** *Chester;* **7.18** *Irlam;* **7.24** *Derby;* **7.35** *Liverpool* **7.35** *Guide Bridge;* **7.38** *Wigan;* **7.40** *ECS;* **7.50** *Cheadle Heath;* **7.55** *ECS;* **8.00** *Lowton St. Mary's;* **8.15** *Cheadle Heath;* **8.25** *Sheffield;* **8.30** *Liverpool;* **8.32** *ECS;* **8.3** *Risley;* **8.38** *ECS;* **8.45 SX** *ECS;* **8.50 SO** *ECS;* **8.55** *Northwich;* **9.00** *St. Pancras;* **9.03** *ECS;* **9.04** *ECS;* **9.10** *ECS;* **9.12** *ECS;* **9.20** *ECS;* **9.30** *Liverpool;* **9.30** *ECS;* **9.3** *Liverpool;* **9.35** *ECS;* **9.48** *Chester;* **9.56** *ECS;* **10.03** *ECS;* **10.05** *Liverpool;* **10.12** *ECS;* **10.25** *Hull (Liverpool-Hull);* **10.27** *ECS;* **10.30** *Liverpool;* **10.40** *Warrington* **10.42** *ECS (to Ardwick from 6.45 ex Leicester);* **10.50** *Sheffield;* **11.10 SO** *Irlam;* **11.20** *ECS* **SX;** **11.35 SX** *Liverpool (Nottingham-Liverpool);* **11.35 SO** *Liverpoo (Nottingham-Liverpool);* **11.42 SX** *ECS;* **11.57** *Chester;* **12.00 SO** *Guide Bridge*

P.M. **12.06** *Stockport;* **12.07 SX** *Irlam;* **12.09 SO** *Aintree;* **12.13 SO** *Irlam;* **12.23 SO** *Buxton;* **12.30** *Liverpool;* **12.30** *Cheadle Heath;* **12.33** *Wigan;* **12.35 S** *Northwich;* **12.37 SO** *ECS;* **12.45 SO** *Cheadle Heath;* **12.50** *Liverpool (Hull-Liverpool);* **12.55 SX** *Irlam;* **12.55** *SO Liverpool;* **1.04** *Sheffield;* **1.07 SX** *ECS;* **1.11** *Irlam* **1.15 SO** *Cheadle Heath;* **1.20 SO** *Chester;* **1.30** *ECS;* **1.30** *Liverpool;* **1.35** *Warrington;* **1.40** *Chester;* **1.45** *Harwich Parkeston Quay (ex Liverpool);* **1.50** *St. Pancras;* **2.0** **SO** *Warrington;* **2.30** *Liverpool;* **2.38** *Liverpool (ex Harwich Parkeston Quay);* **2.48 SO** *Liverpool;* **2.48 SX** *Liverpool;* **2.50** *Derby;* **2.53 SO** *ECS;* **2.55** *ECS;* **3.3** *Liverpool;* **3.33** *Wigan;* **3.35** *Cheadle Heath;* **3.45** *Chester;* **4.00** *St. Pancras;* **4.03** *Sheffield;* **4.05** *Irlam;* **4.15** *Guide Bridge;* **4.17** *ECS;* **4.28** *Chester;* **4.30** *Liverpool;* **4.3** *Nottingham (ex Liverpool);* **4.36 SX** *Stockport;* **4.37 SX** *Irlam;* **4.40 SX** *Northwich;* **4.45 SO** *Irlam;* **4.57 SX** *Aintree;* **5.00 SX** *Cheadle Heath;* **5.07** *Chester;* **5.1** *Stockport;* **5.12 SX** *Irlam;* **5.22 SX** *Buxton;* **5.30** *Liverpool;* **5.30** *Cheadle Heath;* **5.33** *Warrington;* **5.35** *Hull (ex Liverpool);* **5.40 SX** *Chester;* **5.43 SX** *Guide Bridge;* **5.4** **SX** *Irlam;* **5.55** *St. Pancras;* **6.00 SX** *Cheadle Heath;* **6.00 SO** *Chester;* **6.05** *Wigan;* **6.15 SX** *Northwich;* **6.30** *Liverpool;* **6.30 SX** *Cheadle Heath;* **6.35** *Irlam;* **6.40 S** *Chester;* **6.40 SO** *Northwich;* **6.45** *Sheffield;* **6.50 SX** *ECS;* **6.52 SX** *ECS;* **7.05** *ECS;* **7.10** *Wigan;* **7.20 SO** *Chester;* **7.25 FO** *ECS;* **7.30** *Liverpool;* **7.35** *Derby;* **7.4** *Warrington;* **8.10** *Liverpool (ex Hull);* **8.20** *Chester;* **8.30** *Wigan;* **8.45 FO** *ECS;* **9.05** *ECS;* **9.10** *Irlam;* **9.30** *Liverpool;* **9.30** *Sheffield;* **9.40** *Warrington;* **9.42** *ECS;* **9.4** *Cuddington* **10.10** *Cheadle Heath;* **10.18** *ECS;* **10.30** *Liverpool;* **10.30 SO** *ECS;* **10.40** *Northwich;* **11.00 SX** *ECS;* **11.00** *Warrington;* **11.25 SO** *ECS;* **11.45 SX** *ECS*

115. Longsight, c.1955. The name 'Longsight' had a magnetic appeal for train-spotters of all ages from all parts, particularly south Manchester. As the "shed" that provided the motive power requirements of London Road "western" or London Midland side, it was usually stocked with a good few named engines. This picture, taken in the mid-1950s, views the scene from the down platform looking towards Manchester. To the right is the complex containing the locomotive depot and carriage servicing facilities. Alongside No. 1 signal box is a *Caprotti* valve geared "Black Five", whilst an unidentified "Jubilee" locomotive, coaled up, awaits departure for London Road where it will back onto its waiting train. Spreading across the scene is a splendid LNWR signal gantry, the robust semaphores being a feature of the line right up to the commencement of electrification in 1958.

Photo: G. H. Platt

Appendix 5 — **LONDON ROAD — Working Time Table 8th June to 20th September 1953**

DEPARTURES — A.M. **12.2 SX** *Euston via Stoke;* **12.10** *Stockport Parcels;* **12.15 SO** *Paignton;* **12.35** *Penzance (Plymouth SO);* **1.0 SO** *Euston via Stoke;* **1.10** *Chester Newspapers;* **2.50** *Crewe;* **5.25** *Uttoxeter via Leek;* **5.50** *Crewe;* **6.50** *Stafford via Stoke;* **7.5** *Wilmslow via Styal;* **7.15** *Crewe;* **7.27** *Buxton;* **7.37 SX** *Wilmslow via Styal;* **7.40 SX** *Macclesfield;* **8.0** *Crewe, Euston (SX) Birmingham (SO);* **8.10 SO** *Penzance;* **8.20** *Euston via Stoke;* **8.30 SX** *Birmingham;* **8.30 SO** *Euston via Stoke;* **8.42** *Crewe;* **8.47** *Stafford via Stoke;* **9.0** *Buxton;* **9.10** *Plymouth SX Paignton SO;* **9.25** *Swansea High Street;* **9.45** *Euston;* **9.50** *Wilmslow via Styal;* **10.5** *Euston via Stoke;* **10.15** *Birmingham;* **10.25 SX** *Bournemouth West;* **10.25 SO** *Bournemouth West via Stoke;* **10.38 SO** *Bournemouth West;* **10.50 SO** *Aberystwyth;* **11.0** *Stafford SX, Wolverhampton SO;* **11.10** *Crewe;* **11.55** *Plymouth;* **12 noon SO** *Cardiff.*

P.M. **12.5** *Euston via Stoke;* **12.10** *Buxton;* **12.18 SO** *Macclesfield;* **12.20 SO** *Sandbach via Styal;* **12.27 SX** *Stockport;* **12.38 SO** *Wilmslow via Styal;* **12.48** *Birmingham via Stoke;* **12.48 SX** *Wilmslow via Styal;* **12.50 SO** *Buxton;* **12.52 SO** *Uttoxeter;* **1.0 SX** *Uttoxeter;* **1.10 SO** *Wilmslow via Styal;* **1.18** *Crewe;* **1.25 SO** *Buxton;* **1.40 SO** *Macclesfield;* **1.55 FO** *Euston via Stoke;* **2.0 SO** *Wilmslow via Styal;* **2.5 SX** *Euston via Stoke;* **2.10 SO** *Euston via Stoke;* **2.20 SO** *Euston via Stoke;* **2.28 SO** *ECS Chelford Sidings (ex-Euston);* **2.50** *Uttoxeter via Leek;* **3.05** *Birmingham;* **3.15 FSO** *Plymouth;* **3.38 SO** *ECS Chelford Sidings (ex-Euston);* **3.45 SX** *Buxton;* **4.0 SX** *Buxton;* **4.5** *Euston via Stoke;* **4.20 SX** *Stoke;* **4.35** *Birmingham;* **4.30 SX** *Crewe;* **4.45 SX** *Buxton;* **4.51 SX** *Whaley Bridge;* **4.51 SO** *ECS Hazel Grove (ex-Aberystwyth);* **4.55** *Macclesfield;* **5.5 SX** *Buxton;* **5.11** *Crewe;* **5.17 SX** *Stafford via Stoke;* **5.17 SX** *Disley;* **5.22 SX** *Stoke;* **5.22 SX** *Wilmslow via Styal;* **5.30 SX** *Chelford;* **5.40 SX** *Buxton;* **5.40 SX** *Macclesfield;* **5.50** *Euston;* **5.50 SX** *Buxton;* **5.53 SX** *Wilmslow via Styal;* **6.0 SX** *Crewe;* **6.0 SO** *ECS Styal (ex-Exeter);* **6.10 SX** *Wilmslow via Styal;* **6.15 SX** *Cresswell;* **6.20** *Buxton;* **6.42 SO** *ECS Handforth Sidings (ex-Euston);* **7.0** *Buxton;* **7.5** *Macclesfield SX Stoke SO;* **7.10** *Cardiff;* **7.35 SO** *ECS Hazel Grove (ex-Hastings);* **7.45** *Birmingham via Stoke;* **8.15** *Crewe;* **8.20** *Buxton;* **8.42** *Blythe Bridge SX, Uttoxeter SO;* **9.6 SX** *Buxton;* **9.16 SO** *Euston-Newspapers;* **9.25 FO** *Newquay;* **9.30** *Macclesfield;* **9.37** *Crewe;* **10.0** *Wilmslow via Styal;* **10.18 SO** *Stoke;* **10.27** *Crewe-Mails;* **10.33 SX** *Euston-Parcels;* **10.37 FX** *Buxton;* **10.39 FO** *Bournemouth;* **10.55 SX** *Macclesfield;* **11.5 SO** *Stockport;* **11.15 FO** *Penzance;* **11.25 FO** *Euston;* **11.30** *Crewe-Newspapers;* **11.40 FO** *Hastings via Stoke;* **11.55** *Crewe.*

LONDON ROAD—ARRIVALS

A.M. **1.28 MX** *12.41 ex Crewe;* **1.30 MO** *12.41 ex Crewe;* **2.32 MX** *10.45pm ex Euston;* **3.10 MX** *2.9 Parcels ex Crewe;* **3.17 MO** *2.22 Mails ex Crewe;* **3.37 MX** *2.42 Mails ex Crewe;* **4.35** *12.40 ex Euston;* **4.50 SO** *4.40pm FO ex Penzance;* **5.0 MSX** *10.0pm FSX Parcels from Euston via Stoke;* **5.32** *5.15 ex Stockport;* **5.37 MX** *3.35 Parcels from Stafford via Stoke;* **6.6 SO** *10.0 FO Parcels from Euston via Stoke;* **6.8** *4.45pm SX Penzance;* **12.10 MO** *ex Bristol;* **6.48 MX** *5.15 Parcels ex Crewe;* **6.38** *5.50 ex Macclesfield;* **6.53** *6.18 ex Alderley Edge via Styal;* **7.23 SX** *6.47 ex Alderley Edge via Styal;* **7.36** *5.25 ex Blythe Bridge;* **7.41 SX** *7.0 ex Whaley Bridge;* **7.50 SX** *7.10 ex Macclesfield;* **7.51 SO** *6.50 ex Buxton;* **7.57** *6.45 ex Crewe;* **8.13 SX** *7.9 ex Buxton;* **8.24** *7.39 ex Macclesfield;* **8.29** *7.30 ex Buxton;* **8.33** *7.23 ex Crewe;* **8.37** *6.0 ex Stafford via Stoke;* **8.45** *7.50 ex Buxton;* **8.53** *7.5 ex Stoke via Tunstall;* **9.8** *7.50 ex Crewe;* **9.1 SX** *8.20 ex Buxton;* **9.3 SX** *8.33 ex Chelford to Stretford;* **9.8** *7.50 ex Crewe via Stockport;* **9.13** *8.20 SO ex Buxton;* **8.37** *ex Whaley Bridge;* **9.32** *8.34 ex Buxton;* **9.38** *6.52 ex Stafford via Stoke;* **9.48** *9.5 ex Buxton;* **9.53** *7.10 ex Birmingham via Crewe;* **10.22** *8.15 ex Uttoxeter;* **10.29 SX** *9.13 ex Crewe;* **10.29 SO** *7.0 ex Birmingham via Crewe;* **10.36 SO** *ECS 10.50 to Aberystwyth;* **10.35 SX** *9.52 ex Crewe via Stockport;* **11.13** *8.40 ex Uttoxeter;* **11.21 SX** *10.45 ex Alderley Edge via Styal;* **11.18** *10.20 ex Buxton;* **11.27** *10.45 ex Crewe via Stockport;* **11.38 SO** *9.20 ex Birmingham;* **11.40 SO ECS** *for 12 noon to Cardiff;* **11.43 SX** *11.1 ex Crewe via Stockport.*

P.M. **12.39 SX** *8.30 ex Euston;* **12.50 SO** *8.45 ex Euston via Stoke;* **12.55 SO** *12.10 ex Crewe via Stockport;* **1.6 MO** *9.35 ex Euston;* **1.12 SO** *9.35 ex Euston;* **1.19** *11.55 ex Stoke;* **1.24 SO** *8.38 ex Cardiff;* **1.27 FO** *ECS for 1.55 to Euston;* **1.25 SX** *9.45 ex Euston via Stoke;* **1.39** *8.55 ex Cardiff;* **1.46 SO** *ECS for 2.10 to Euston;* **1.49 SX** *1.32 ex Stockport;* **2.1 SO** *12.8 ex Cresswell;* **2.4 SX** *12.53 ex Crewe;* **2.9 SX** *1.38 ex Wilmslow via Styal;* **2.17 SX** *1.10 ex Buxton;* **2.13 SO** *1.3 ex Crewe;* **2.16 SO** *9.45 ex Euston via Stoke;* **2.33 FSX** *12.10 ex Birmingham;* **2.35 FSO** *12.10 ex Birmingham;* **2.48 SO** *2.20 ex Wilmslow via Stockport;* **3.21 SX** *1.45 ex Stoke;* **3.29 SO** *11.37 ex Euston via Stoke;* **3.30 SX** *11.45 ex Euston via Crewe;* **3.42 SO** *11.45 ex Euston via Crewe;* **4.1 SX** *2.53 ex Crewe;* **4.6 SO** *1.45 ex Birmingham;* **4.9 SX** *2.20 ex Stafford via Stoke;* **4.20 SX** *3.37 ex Crewe;* **4.25 SO** *12.37 ex Euston via Stoke;* **4.41 SO** *11.0 ex Aberystwyth;* **4.46 SX** *4.5 ex Macclesfield;* **4.48 SO** *4.0 ex Crewe;* **4.58 SX** *4.40 ex Stockport;* **5.18 MFSO** *9.5 ex Paignton;* **5.30** *11.15 ex Swansea High Street;* **5.35 SO** *10.4 ex Exeter;* **5.40 SO** *9.45 ex Bournemouth West via Stoke;* **6.5 SO** *4.52 ex Crewe via Styal;* **5.58 SX** *3.34 ex Stafford via Stoke;* **6.0 SO** *3.41 ex Stafford via Stoke;* **6.10** *5.10 ex Crewe;* **6.19** *3.50 ex Birmingham via Crewe;* **6.31 SO** *5.55 ex Wilmslow via Stockport;* **6.35 SX** *5.55 ex Wilmslow via Stockport;* **6.3 FO** *2.38 ex Euston via Crewe;* **6.35 SO** *2.38 ex Euston via Stoke;* **6.49** *5.40 ex Buxton;* **6.46** *2.45 ex Euston via Stoke;* **7.3 SO** *7.50 ex Newquay;* **7.13** *5.15 ex Stoke;* **7.9 SO** *3.0 ex Euston via Stoke;* **7.16 SO** *12.30 ex Hastings via Stoke;* **7.20** *6.10 ex Crewe;* **7.24** *6.35 ex Crewe;* **7.45 SO** *6.40 ex Buxton;* **7.49 SX** *6.40 ex Buxton;* **7.56** *3.45 ex Euston via Stoke;* **8.23 SX** *7.35 ex Macclesfield;* **8.41 FX** *7.53 ex Crewe;* **8.41 FO** *6.5 ex Birmingham;* **8.56** *8.25 ex Wilmslow via Styal;* **9.20** *8.10 ex Crewe;* **9.25 FX** *7.30 ex Stoke;* **9.33 SO** *8.27 ex Buxton;* **9.40 FSX** *8.32 ex Buxton;* **9.40 SO** *6.0 ex Euston via Crewe;* **9.30 SX** *6.0 ex Euston via Crewe;* **9.49 SX** *8.57 ex Crewe;* **9.58 SO** *4.40 ex Cardiff;* **10.06 SO** *12.30 ex Paignton;* **10.15** *4.59 ex Rugby SX, 6.24 ex Birmingham SO;* **10.31** *10.0 ex Wilmslow via Styal;* **10.50 FX** *9.45 ex Buxton;* **10.59 FX** *9.50 ex Crewe;* **11.45** *11.45 ex Stoke;* **11.58 SO** *11.0 ex Buxton.*

116. Levenshulme North, 1955. Levenshulme was at one time the second station out of London Road on the Manchester to Crewe line via Stockport. Here one has a uninterrupted view of the four track formation looking down towards Slade Lane Junction. The station first saw light of day in August 1842 shortly after the Manchester an Birmingham Railway opened its line from Travis Street to Heaton Norris. Continuing increases in traffic resulted in the 1884 quadrupling of the section between Ardwick an Heaton Norris, Levenshulme being completely rebuilt. In this view we see "Jubilee" No. 45582 *Central Provinces* speeding along the up fast line with a lightweight express c four coaches. The LNWR signal box and lower-quadrant signals, sturdy time-served sentinels, were all swept away by the Heaton Norris re-signalling scheme of 1955.
Photo: R. E. Ge

Appendix 6 — **MANCHESTER VICTORIA — Working Time Table 6th October 1947. Central Division Section 1**
DEPARTURES A.M. 12.30 *(11 MID) News and Parcels to Leeds City;* **1.00 MX** *17 Periodicals to Oldham Road;* **1.15 SO; 2.12 WFO** *Loco Stores Van;* **2.25** *(11 M) New and Parcels to Leeds City;* **3.17** *(11 M) Mail to Oldham and Bury;* **4.20** *(5) Express to Normanton;* **5.07** *(6) All stations Rochdale via Moston;* **5.10** *(9) Stalybridge;* **5.15** *(16 Colne;* **5.17** *(7) Royton;* **5.55** *(9) Stalybridge;* **6.05** *(8) Bolton via Oldham;* **6.26** *(4) Ramsbottom* **(SX)** *Bury* **(SO); 6.38** *(8) Castleton* **(SX)** *Rochdale* **(SO)** *via Oldham;* **6.45** *(16 Stockport;* **6.48** *(14) All stations to Normanton;* **6.50** *(9) Stalybridge;* **7.04** *(6) Middleton;* **7.15** *(8) Rochdale via Oldham;* **7.26** *(6) Middleton;* **7.33** *(13) Rochdale via Moston* **7.35** *(9) Stalybridge;* **7.40** *(7) Rochdale via Oldham;* **7.40** *(4) Bacup via Heywood;* **7.55** *(6) Middleton;* **8.00** *(7) Royton;* **8.18** *(9) Stalybridge;* **8.18** *(13) Halifax (ex 7.0 Southport);* **8.22** *(8) Royton;* **8.43** *(15) Bury (Knowsley St.);* **8.46** *(7) Rochdale via Oldham;* **8.55** *[13)* **SO** *Scarborough;* **9.05** *(9) Stalybridge;* **9.10** *(7) Rochdale via Oldham* **9.25** *(13) Leeds (ex Liverpool Exch.);* **9.38** *(15) Stockport (ex 8.00 Colne);* **9.45** *(8) Royton;* **10.00** *(13) York via Todmorden;* **10.40** *[6) Rochdale via Oldham;* **11.05** *(8) Shaw* **11.30** *(7) Royton;* **11.30** *(13) Newcastle, ex 10.30 Liverpool Exchange;* **11.55** *(4) Bacup via Heywood;* **12.02** *(7)* **SX** *Royton.*
P.M. 12.02 *(8)* **SO** *Bolton via Oldham;* **12.05** *(9)* **SO** *Stalybridge;* **12.10** *(13)* **SO** *York;* **12.10** *(6)* **SO** *Royton;* **12.12** *(4)* **SO** *Middleton;* **12.19** *(9) Stalybridge, Mossley* **SO** **12.25** *(13) Liverpool Exchange – Leeds;* **12.30** *(8)* **SX** *Royton;* **12.30** *(9)* **SO** *Royton;* **12.33** *(4)* **SO** *Bury (Bolton St.);* **12.37** *(6)* **SO** *Middleton;* **12.50** *(15)* **SO** *Bolton t Normanton;* **12.53** *(8)* **SO** *Royton;* **1.05** *(8)* **SX** *Rochdale (via Oldham);* **1.05** *(7)* **SO** *Rochdale (via Oldham);* **1.09** *(9) Stalybridge;* **1.16** *(4)* **SO** *Bacup;* **1.47** *(6)* **SO** *Middleton;* **2.05** *(7)* **SX** *Royton;* **2.05** *(8)* **SO** *Royton;* **2.25** *(13) Southport-Bradford;* **2.29** *(thro' rd)* **SO 12.53** *Blackpool Cen.-Leeds City;* **2.55** *(8)* **SX** *Rochdale (via Oldham)* **2.58** *(7)* **SO** *Oldham Mumps;* **3.20** *(7)* **SX** *Shaw;* **3.20** *(13) Liverpool Exchange-Leeds;* **3.25** *(9)* **SO** *Shaw;* **3.30** *(9) Mossley;* **3.55** *(8)* **SX** *Royton;* **4.08** *(7,* **SX** *Rochdale (via Oldham);* **4.08** *(8)* **SO** *Rochdale (via Oldham);* **4.15** *(6) Middleton;* **4.18** *(thro' rd)* **SO** *Blackpool (North) to Desford;* **4.18** *(9)* **SX** *Stalybridge;* **4.22** *(thro rd)* **SO** *(Blackpool Cen. to Leeds City);* **4.25** *(8)* **SX** *Royton;* **4.25** *(7)* **SO** *Royton;* **4.28** *(9)* **SO** *Stalybridge;* **4.37** *(13) Halifax;* **4.50** *(7)* **SX** *Royton;* **4.50** *(8)* **SO** *Royton;* **5.0** *(13) Bacup;* **5.03** *(10)* **SX** *Stalybridge;* **5.03** *(9)* **SO** *Stalybridge;* **5.06** *(6)* **SX** *Rochdale (via Oldham);* **5.07** *(thro' rd)* **SO** *Blackpool North to Derby;* **5.09** *(9)* **SX** *Middleton* **5.09** *(6)* **SO** *Middleton;* **5.12** *(13) Colne to Stockport;* **5.17** *(5)* **SX** *Bury Knowsley St. & Horwich;* **5.17** *(4)* **SO** *Bury Knowsley St. & Horwich;* **5.18** *(8) Rochdale via Oldham* **5.25** *(13) Liverpool (Exchange) to Leeds;* **5.30** *(7) Royton;* **5.35** *(15) Todmorden;* **5.40** *(9) Mossley;* **5.43** *(thro' rd)* **SO** *Blackpool North to Sheffield;* **5.45** *(8)* **SX** *Royton;* **5.5** *(13) Pendleton (Broad St.) to Normanton;* **6.00** *(7)* **SX** *Rochdale via Oldham;* **6.00** *(8)* **SO** *Rochdale via Oldham;* **6.03** *(6)* **SX** *Middleton;* **6.12** *(4) Bacup;* **6.27** *(5)* **SX** *Royton* **6.27** *(7)* **SO** *Royton;* **6.52** *(7)* **SX** *Oldham (Mumps);* **7.05** *(4) Bacup;* **7.15** *(8) Royton;* **7.30** *(9) Stalybridge;* **7.30** *(13) Liverpool (Exchange)-Newcastle;* **7.40** *(13) Leeds;* **7.4** *(7) Rochdale (via Oldham);* **8.07** *(thro' rd)* **SO** *Fish 5.30 Wyre Dock-Stockport T.D.;* **8.15** *(17)* **SO** *Parcels to Stockport;* **8.20** *(17)* **SX** *Parcels to Normanton;* **8.25** *(5)* **SX** *Bacup;* **8.25** *(4)* **SO** *Bacup;* **8.33** *(7) Rochdale via Oldham;* **8.40** *(9) Stalybridge;* **9.00** *(13)* **FO** *Paignton;* **9.05** *(6) Middleton Junction;* **9.10** *(8)* **SO** *Rochdale via Oldham;* **9.1** *(11 M) Express Newspaper & Parcels to York;* **9.18** *(4)* **SX** *Bacup;* **9.18** *(5)* **SO** *Bacup;* **9.20** *(10) Stalybridge;* **9.26** *ECS Southport;* **9.32** *(13) Liverpool (Exchange to Leeds)* **9.35** *(7) Rochdale via Oldham;* **9.53** *(9)* **SX** *Royton;* **9.53** *(7)* **SO** *Royton;* **10.17** *(4) Bury Bolton St.;* **10.20** *(13)* **FO** *Paignton;* **10.20** *(17)* **SX** *Bolton to Stockport Parcels;* **10.2** *(8) Royton;* **10.25** *(15) Colne;* **10.30** *(17)* **SO** *Sowerby Bridge;* **10.30** *(13)* **SX** *Todmorden;* **10.35** *(9) Stalybridge;* **10.40** *(4)* **SO** *Bacup;* **10.50** *(6)* **SX** *Rochdale (via Oldham)* **10.50** *(8)* **SO** *Rochdale (via Oldham);* **11.15** *(13)* **FO** *Paignton;* **11.25** *(16)* **SX** *Parcels & Fish Blackpool (North)-Leeds.*

Appendix 7 — **MANCHESTER VICTORIA – Working Time Table 6th October 1947. Central Division Section 3**
DEPARTURES A.M. 12.50 *(12)* **MX** *to Manchester Exchange (Parcels from Stockport);* **3.05** *(11 MID) to Blackpool (North);* **3.15** *(11 MID)* **MX** *to Southpor (Newspapers);* **3.30** *(11 MID)* **MO** *to Southport (Newspapers);* **4.10** *Colne;* **4.20** *(16)* **SO** *Blackpool (North) Parcels;* **4.35** *(11 MID) Hellifield;* **5.20** *(11) Bolton (T.S.);* **5.2** *(11 MID) Southport (via Daisy Hill);* **6.05** *(12) Liverpool (Exchange)-Local;* **6.15** *(15) Burscough Bridge;* **6.45** *(12) Blackpool (North) & Fleetwood;* **6.50** *(15) Colne;* **7.0** *(15) Atherton (Cen.);* **7.10** *(12)* **SX** *Preston;* **7.55** *(14) Southport;* **8.00** *(15) Accrington;* **8.05** *(12) Horwich;* **8.25** *(11) Liverpool (Exchange)–from Bradford;* **8.30** *(11 MID, Blackpool (North)–from Stockport;* **8.35** *(13) Hellifield;* **8.38** *(14) Skipton;* **8.45** *(12) Blackpool (Cen.);* **8.58** *(11) Southport;* **9.12** *(11) Southport;* **9.20** *(12) Hellifield;* **9.3** *(11 MID) Glasgow (Cen.);* **9.28** *(12) Liverpool (Exchange)–from Leeds/Bradford;* **9.40** *(14) Colne;* **9.40** *(14)* **SO** *Barrow;* **9.50** *(11 MID) Workington;* **9.55** *(12) Preston* **10.15** *(15) Wigan (Wallgate);* **10.25** *(11 MID) Blackpool (North & Central) & Fleetwood;* **10.30** *(12) Southport;* **11.03** *(11)* **SX** *Liverpool (Exchange)–from Leeds/Bradford* **11.15** *(12) Blackpool (North) & Fleetwood;* **11.25** *(11 MID)* **SO** *Southport;* **11.40** *(12)* **SO** *Blackpool (Cen.);* **11.48** *(14)* **SO** *Hellifield;* **12.02** *(13)* **SO** *Bolton (T.S.);* **12.0** *(12) Blackpool (Cen.);* **12.08** *(14)* **SO** *Wigan (Wallgate);* **12.15** *(11)* **SO** *Southport (arr. 1.13);* **12.15** *(11)* **WSX** *Southport (arr. 1.17);* **12.15** *(11)* **WO** *Southport (arr. 1.26)* **12.20** *(12)* **SO** *Blackpool (North);* **12.22** *(15) Colne;* **12.27** *(14)* **SO** *Wigan;* **12.30** *(12)* **SO** *Hellifield;* **12.35** *(11 MID) Liverpool (Exchange)–from Leeds/Bradford;* **.45** *(1 MID)* **SO** *Southport;* **12.45** *(15)* **SX** *Hellifield;* **12.45** *(14)* **SO** *Hellifield;* **12.50** *(12)* **SO** *Blackpool (Cen.)*
P.M. 1.00 *(12)* **SO** *Blackpool (North);* **1.03** *(14)* **SO** *Bolton (T.S.);* **1.07** *(15)* **SX** *Southport;* **1.07** *(11)* **SO** *Southport;* **1.15** *(11 MID)* **SO** *Fleetwood;* **1.25** *(12)* **SO** *Barrow* **1.40** *(12) Blackpool North & Fleetwood;* **1.50** *(11 MID) Southport;* **2.05** *(14) Skipton;* **2.10** *(11) Wigan (Wallgate);* **2.15** *(14) Bolton (T.S.);* **2.50** *(12) Liverpool (Exchange (from Leeds/Bradford);* **2.55** *(14) Stockport to Colne;* **3.12** *(15)* **SO** *Southport;* **3.15** *(11 MID) Blackpool (Central & North);* **3.17** *(12) Blackpool (Central);* **3.23** *(14)* **SX** *Colne;* **3.35** *(15)* **SX** *Bacup;* **3.38** *(12) Blackburn;* **4.03** *(14)* **SX** *Wigan (Wallgate);* **4.10** *(11) Southport;* **4.10** *(12) Blackpool (North);* **4.16** *(12) Preston;* **4.23** *(14) Liverpoo (Exchange)–from Newcastle;* **4.26** *(12) Blackpool (Express);* **4.37** *(12)* **SX** *Hellifield;* **4.37** *(11) Southport;* **4.43** *(15) Horwich;* **4.46** *(15)* **SO** *Wigan (Wallgate);* **4.55** *(12)* **SX** *Blackpool (North);* **5.00** *(12)* **SX** *Southport;* **5.03** *(11)* **SX** *Blackpool (Cen.);* **5.05** *(14)* **SX** *Hindley;* **5.15** *(12) Blackpool (Cen.);* **5.18** *(14) Bolton (T.S.);* **5.46** *(11 MID)* **SX** *Blackpool (Cen.);* **5.22** *(12)* **SX** *Southport;* **5.25** *(11)* **SX** *Wigan (Wallgate);* **5.30** *(15)* **SO** *Wigan (Wallgate);* **5.35** *(11)* **SX** *Liverpool (Exchange)–from Leeds/Bradford;* **5.4** *(12) Southport;* **5.40** *(14)* **SX** *Hellifield;* **5.45** *(15) Liverpool (Exchange)–Local;* **5.45** *(12)* **SX** *Blackpool (North) & Fleetwood;* **5.55** *(12)* **SX** *Blackpool (Cen.);* **6.00** *(14)* **SX** *Southport;* **6.10** *(11 MID)* **SX** *Southport (Express);* **6.12** *(12) Preston;* **6.15** *(15)* **SX** *Wigan (Wallgate);* **6.23** *(12)* **SO** *Colne;* **6.30** *(14) Hellifield;* **6.38** *(11)* **SX** *Liverpoo (Exchange)–From Leeds & Bradford;* **6.45** *(15)* **SO** *Southport;* **7.03** *(12) Blackpool (North & Cen.) & Fleetwood;* **7.05** *(11)* **SX** *Southport;* **7.15** *(12) Bolton (T.S.);* **7.22** *(15, Liverpool (Exchange)–Local;* **7.34** *(12) Stockport to Colne;* **8.00** *(15) Southport;* **8.05** *(14) Colne;* **8.15** *(12) Blackpool (Cen. & North) & Fleetwood;* **8.15** *(11) Liverpoo (Exchange)–Local;* **9.00** *(14) Southport (From Leeds & Bradford);* **9.05** *(12) Heysham;* **9.08** *(13) Southport;* **9.10** *(11) Blackburn;* **9.20** *(15) Colne;* **9.35** *(12) Liverpoo (Exchange)–From Newcastle;* **9.39** *(11)* **SX** *Horwich;* **10.00** *(14) Blackpool (Cen.) & Fleetwood;* **10.05** *(15) Wigan (Wallgate);* **10.15** *(12)* **SO** *Southport;* **10.45** *(14, Atherton;* **10.50** *(12) Blackburn;* **11.05** *(14)* **FO** *Fleetwood;* **11.10** *(14)* **SO** *Wigan (Wallgate);* **11.15** *(12)* **SO** *Bolton (T.S.)*